SINGLE
IN PORTLAND

Living Fully on Your Own

HARRY H. STEIN

Published by Historical-Media Services, 1926 Southeast Hemlock, Portland, Oregon 97214, in cooperation with Coast to Coast Books.

Library of Congress Cataloging in Publication Data
Stein, Harry H., 1938-
  Single in Portland.

  Bibliography: p.
  Includes index.
  1. Single people—Oregon—Portland Metropolitan Area—Directories. 2. Portland Metropolitan Area (Or.)—Directories. 3. Quality of Life—Oregon—Portland Metropolitan Area—Directories. I. Title. HQ800.4.U62P677 1983   305'.90652
83-14262 ISBN 0-9602664-5-3

CONTENTS

4
SINGLES GROUPS AND EVENTS

5
BARS, CLUBS, AND DANCING

6
MORE DELIGHTS

7
SINGLE PLUS

8
CLOSE ENCOUNTERS

PREFACE

I gladly acknowledge aid from many individuals and organizations. Innumerable single people told me about their experiences, answered questions, made suggestions, filled out questionnaires, and encouraged me repeatedly as I worked on this book. Promised anonymity, they will recognize in these pages how important they have been.

Leaders and staffs of hundreds of organizations, clubs, and agencies cooperated fully when asked about their activities, goals, and makeup. They are no more responsible for what I did with their information than are the many others who tried to make this book useful.

Happily, there are several I can identify, for this book reflects their talented contributions, too. Mark Beach heads the list. As co-publisher of Coast to Coast Books, he creatively shaped this book at every turn. It was a pleasure to continue a colleagueship with him and Kathleen Ryan which resulted earlier in our book *Portland: A Pictorial History*.

Betty Daggett, Director of Counseling at SOLO Center, influenced the book from its outline to final stage. In conversations and while commenting on both versions of my manuscript, she shared her compassionate understanding of singles and their lives in this region.

Three other professionals usefully read the first version and talked about their knowledge of single life: Kate Cooper, a counselor, Dr. Michael Rolfson of Marylhurst College, and social worker/teacher Jack West. Two counselors of singles, Steve Regner and Dr. Betty Joy Bryant, also provided information.

Randi Sulkin, now a reporter in Alaska, suggested valuable editorial changes. Martha Stuckey and Susan Page intelligently edited the final manuscript. Corinna Campbell expertly designed the book and cover. Patti Morris and Martin White of Irish Setter made nice improvements while carefully setting type. Katherine J. McCanna, who has helped many an Oregon writer, and Walter H. Crandall enthusiastically suggested how best to put this book into as many hands as possible. Dr. Stephen M. Johnson, from the University of Oregon psychology faculty, allowed me to quote from his *First Person Singular*.

While information in these pages is as accurate as possible, things change. Events, activities, even organizations come and go, changing addresses, phone numbers, meeting times and places. Groups strike out in new directions with new people. Call or write ahead to verify information. The contact lets you learn more about them, too.

HELP MAKE THE NEXT EDITION BETTER

What would you like to see new or different in the next edition of the book?

First, tell me about events, organizations, clubs, places which I missed or misunderstood or which have changed somehow (how?) since this edition. Please tell me whom I should call or write: name; address; town; and phone number. I need to verify this information.

Second, what from your experience is worth including in the next edition? I will keep your experience anonymous if I use it in the next edition. Just tell me your age and sex and any other relevant characteristic, such as single parent.

Please send your note to Harry H. Stein, c/o Coast To Coast Books, 2934 NE 16th, Portland OR 97212.

Thank you.

JULY, 1983

S	M	T	W	T	F	S
					1	2
3	4	5	6	7	8	9
10	11	12	13	14	15	16
17	18	19	20	21	22	23
24/31	25	26	27	28	29	30

LAST MONTH

June						1983
S	M	T	W	T	F	S
			1	2	3	4
5	6	7	8	9	10	11
12	13	14	15	16	17	18
19	20	21	22	23	24	25
26	27	28	29	30		

NEXT MONTH

August						1983
S	M	T	W	T	F	S
	1	2	3	4	5	6
7	8	9	10	11	12	13
14	15	16	17	18	19	20
21	22	23	24	25	26	27
28	29	30	31			

SUNDAY
184/181
3
LAST QUARTER

Brunch in park with the gang 11:30

MONDAY
185/180
4

Independence Day

join neighbors at Holiday Picnic — bring salad!

TUESDAY
186/179
5

Tennis Lesson

WEDNESDAY
187/178
6

Make movie date for Sat.

THURSDAY
188/177
7

Write those letters!

FRIDAY
189/176
8

Canoe Club program

SATURDAY
190/175
9

Movie 9:00

JUL. 3 TO 9, 1983

1
LOOKING AHEAD

WHERE TO?

Single In Portland is about where to go and what to do if you want to have fun, meet new people, and enrich your life. It identifies sources in the four-county metropolitan area for social, emotional, institutional, and person-to-person support.

This book also is about confidants, companions, and lovers, and the importance of building networks of friends. It is about recognizing, giving, doing, and getting things as a single and, always, as a person.

It touches briefly on housing, jobs, and emergencies. It points out ways to stay informed about events and places, about Portland, and about single living. Every chapter also contains material—sometimes quite a lot—for those who are paired.

In short, the book is meant to aid singles—pairs, too—find new resources and expand familiar ones in the Portland metropolitan area: Oregon's Multnomah, Washington, and Clackamas counties and Washington's Clark County. The book might as easily have been titled *Portland Alone* or *Portland Together*.

It is not simply a compendium of organizations and phone numbers. I include many comments and ideas—mine and others'—on the quality of single life, and throw in a friendly suggestion now and then.

Let me tell you how the book developed; that's the best way I know to explain its orientation. It began with a question.

A friend had dropped by my house. We chatted about a number of things and then he asked me, "Where can I go to meet women?" I told him about a dozen or so places that were new to him, all the time asking myself, "How can he not know about these places? He's lived in Portland ten years longer than I have." Even after he had left, I kept thinking about his question.

Women friends would ask, "Where are all the decent single men?" The question kept surfacing whenever we talked about being single. "All around you," I would answer, knowing I sounded too flip—we all knew things were more complicated than *that*.

As we talked as single people, we realized that we wanted more than just to meet people or even that "special person." We found ourselves using phrases such as "a good life as a person, not just as a single person" and "creative involvement with life." We were talking about building and maintaining rich lives. The idea for this book began to develop. And as I talked about the book, almost everybody had suggestions.

Tell us, singles said, about places, groups, and events besides bars. Describe happenings and places outside, not just inside the City of Portland. Give readers the flavor of places, groups, and events. Be sure to show them where and how to get information on their own.

Describe their low- and high-risk choices, a social worker advised. If singles are reluctant to try something, good information and descriptions could help them want to join in. "Give singles the courage to take the plunge," a 66-year-old man advocated.

So be upbeat and encouraging, and at the same time be realistic and critical, I was being told.

And what if they were just lonely? Or faced an emergency? Or wanted to find a better job? Suppose they preferred the company of singles? Or liked instead a mix of singles and couples? Or wanted to be around only those of similar age? Or with people of different ages?

Suggestions multiplied. What could I indicate to someone new to being single? Anything special readers needed to know as new widows, as single parents, or as singles with a physical or mental disability? Several people asked that I briefly note what other authors have written on the single condition.

They wanted to know what other singles were thinking, experiencing, and doing. "I am single *by choice*, but some are single by default," cautioned a 34-year-old woman. "It's not fair to assume *everyone* who *is* single wants to remain in that state."

All of these suggestions influenced *Single in Portland*.

Happily, Portland has many different ways to satisfy tastes. The area spills over with fine chances to work, love, and create. Natural beauty surrounds us. We can have privacy or the company of others. A wealth of places, groups, institutions, and events compete for our attention. And there is something else. Where other cities foster a competitiveness, a self-protectiveness that keeps people apart, there seems to be an atmosphere around here of openness and warmth that promotes the building of strong human attachments.

"Portland is great because there are so many things to do, and so many models of single people just doing their 'thing' in a positive, self-motivated way," a 29-year-old man told me.

"Portland has lots of single people and hence is a better place for singles than a small town full of families." This 36-year-old woman's sentiment is widely shared here.

I do not necessarily share the attitudes, outlooks, values, or practices of every group represented or everyone quoted in these pages. No one will. All sorts of organizations, places, events, and activities are reviewed for readers to make their own choices.

Some readers surely will know of things I failed to include. Some will know more than I about particular aspects of the single life. (Help remedy these situations by responding to the appeal for fresh information and comments at the front of the book.)

I cast a wide net in this book, because being single has so many different meanings to people. When I use "single" in this book, I mean a person not currently married or cohabiting with another. Being single is a civil status.

It is a term tarnished by social prejudice. Some singles avoid the word because of unhappy past experiences. There are singles who prefer to call themselves widowed, single parents, or just people. These different names, however, do not alter their being single as I use the word.

Other singles use terms like "unattached" or "free agent" because "single" can have uncomplimentary connotations. Every single has heard these stereotypes. Moments of loneliness or unhappiness may trigger the same negative feelings in singles themselves.

Sociologists Cargan and Melko argue in *Singles: Myths and Realities* that negative stereotypes of singles have become widespread popular myths in the United States. Never-married men, according to one myth, are tied to their mothers' apron strings. In other myths, singles are perceived as loners, selfish, irresponsible, or shortsighted, or, for not being married, as failures or misfits.

All these myths conclude that there is something wrong about being single. A 39-year-old Portland woman noted that some women "feel sorry for my 'deprived,' that is, single status. I've learned that's a prejudice not worth arguing over."

Numerous singles mentioned pressure from parents to marry or remarry. "Many conversations with my parents have depressed me," remembered a 34-year-old divorced woman. "They focus on how 'incomplete' or 'empty' my life must be. I focus on how full and exciting it is—mostly because I'm single and can make independent decisions."

Single parents may get similar—or quite opposite—pressure from their children. "Romance in your forties is having your teenage child tell you not to say anything 'weird' or having your teenage daughter advise you not to be a 'prude,'" which might, in either case, "scare him off," a 43-year-old woman remarked.

Then there are the myths, Cargan and Melko added, of singles as great swingers (as compared to the safely married). And many couples operate from myths that singles are happier than they are, or that they are richer, because they have neither spouse nor children to support. (Tell that to single parents and watch the reaction.)

I use the term "single" neutrally to discourage stereotyping

4

and because I believe that singles form no one community with identical interests or characteristics. Singles are alike neither in their singleness nor in their experience of singlehood.

"I used to think that being single was a disease, that it meant there was something wrong with me," said a 29-year-old man. "Now I value it very much and am not likely to give it up. I have so much freedom and choice." A 39-year-old woman said, "Learning that as a single parent I could be independent has been one of the most important lessons of my life."

American singles in numerous surveys overwhelmingly speak of being and feeling "free" as a special advantage of the single status. For Portland area singles, their "freedom" proved to have several overlapping positive meanings. Here is a sampling:

- "the ability to make life decisions—take directions without consulting or negotiating with another person." (24-year-old never-married woman)
- "freedom from commitment, freedom from time restraints, freedom to do things that may seem bizarre or weird to a mate or spouse." (30-year-old divorced man)
- "freedom to come and go and make and live in my mess (and clean it up)." (43-year-old separated man)
- "having my own space whenever I want it to think or rest. I'm able to experience a variety of intimate relationships, deciding when or when not to put my energy there." (29-year-old never-married man)
- freedom to come and go as I please, freedom to make spur-of-the-moment decisions without ties . . . a feeling of independence is present." (31-year-old never-married woman)
- "sexual freedom, more time to pursue activities and friendships" than if married, and "freedom to live the way I want and use my time the way I want." (36-year-old divorced woman)
- "freedom and privacy to do things, go places, meet people, learn, grow, experience, and learn what kind of man and relationship I want and need *without* having ruined a marriage to find out." (34-year-old never-married woman)
- "freedom to grow and develop. I guess I'm looking for a

5

mate who will allow that in married life." (30-year-old never-married man)

Singles living alone testified to its mix of advantages and disadvantages. Some were concerned about personal finances. "Two incomes are better than one," said a 34-year-old woman, although "expenses are often lower for one than for couples." "Living alone is expensive, if you want a nice place," commented another 34-year-old woman. In contrast, a newly separated 43-year-old man found that "it is possible to have a very satisfying social life and not spend lots of money."

Many described aloneness as two-sided emotionally. Although he could "control my space at any time," a 29-year-old man added that "I don't have someone to share my excitements or failures with when I feel I need to do that." Before mentioning how living alone was "a hassle if the car breaks down" and sometimes meant loneliness, a 34-year-old woman waxed ecstatic on the benefits:

> Privacy—peace and quiet—no cigarette smoke—freedom to walk around nude if I feel like it—make noise if I feel like it—use the phone for hours without worrying about disturbing anyone—enjoying quiet time alone—no one's mess but my own.

Being "accountable only to myself" for whatever he did and did not do when living alone also meant to a 30-year-old man "eating alone. Sleeping alone. No one to 'take care of me' if and when I need it."

To a 66-year-old man:

> living alone is the pits. It is a wholly unnatural and disagreeable way to live. Unless I discuss things with other people, I have much more difficulty deciding what I believe or why I believe it. One's sex life becomes disorganized when one lives alone. Not all couples have solved *that* problem.

Single or not, every adult has sometimes known loneliness—that depressed feeling of aloneness. In Simenaueur and Carroll's national survey, *Singles*, 42% of the men and 44% of the women considered it the greatest disadvantage of being single. Among those living alone, 85% lamented the difficulties loneliness introduced into their lives.

Many Portland singles confront loneliness by keeping busy. One 31-year-old woman described herself as "almost burning the candle at both ends. I am active in clubs, organizations, visit friends, invite others to dinner."

A 39-year-old single parent handled her occasional loneliness in "many ways: becoming a hermit and finding resources within myself; reaching out to friends to help me through bad times, or escaping for a while into a good book." A 30-year-old man wrote, "I keep my mind and body occupied, especially my mind, and try to do something that, when I'm finished, I can feel a sense of accomplishment from."

Two 34-year-old women prone to list-making shared some of their ways of coping with loneliness. One wrote:

1. Reach out and make contacts if I need companionship.

2. Develop projects that are fun and fulfilling to do alone.

3. Plan ahead so that if I feel lonely tonight at least something is planned for tomorrow.

4. Go places by myself where I can either meet people or escape (i.e., a movie, play, concert). Occasionally you just have to wallow in it.

The second made similar, if more emphatic, suggestions:

1. *Plan ahead*—make sure on weekends you have something special to look forward to (holidays, too).

2. *Reward yourself*—don't wait for someone else to bring you flowers and champagne; buy them for yourself.

3. *Enjoy your own company*—go out alone and enjoy it.

4. *Take initiative*—I throw lots of Sunday brunches.

A 29-year-old man admitted handling loneliness "sometimes gracefully and sometimes like a rank amateur." Sounds familiar.

There is, then, no one "singles experience" whether we live alone or with another, in how we live alone or with others, in how we appreciate or understand our single status, or in how we handle any loneliness.

Likewise, there is no one "singles scene" in metropolitan Portland. As women or men, singles possess different backgrounds and expectations. We may live with parents or be parents. We may be deep-rooted here or recent arrivals. The never-married, the divorced, the separated, and the widowed all have different histories. Singles are unalike in income, lifestyle, age, health, education, personality, outlook, abilities, and sexual preference.

But in one important way, singles *are* alike—in their humanity. They want meaningful work, security, love, enjoyment, a decent home, peace, a sense of contributing something valuable, satisfaction from sharing, intimacy, companionship, and community and . . . you name it. Single life is life itself.

As one 34-year-old woman suggested, "Being a happy single is being a happy person, which is the same as self-acceptance," liking yourself, and having a "good overall sense of the world."

WHO ARE THE SINGLES?

You may be surprised how many singles live here. The 1980 Census counted over 326,000 singles older than 15 in the four-county Portland metropolitan region. Their median age is 30.4; and 51.3% of them are female. Somewhat more men than women have never married. In the other Census categories of divorced, separated, and widowed, the proportion of women to men is much higher.

On a national scale, the singles population is an increasing segment of the population. Censuses show an increased tendency of Americans to postpone and forego marriage as well as a growing divorce rate. The marriage rate continues its fall. In 1982, 53% of American women between 20 and 24 and 23% between 25 and 30 years old, for instance, have never married. The comparable percentages for men are 72% and 36%, respectively.

The divorce rate has climbed from 47 per thousand married Americans in 1970 to 109 per thousand marrieds in 1981. Single women headed 3.23 million families in 1981. In single-parent families, 18.1% of all American children lived only with their mother and 1.9% lived only with their father in 1981.

Living alone has grown very common. In March 1982, 19.4

million Americans lived alone, a jump of 78% since 1970. In 1981, 23% of American households consisted of persons living alone. Women composed 62% of these households; 56% of them are widowed.

Many living alone are elderly, the 65 and older category increasing by 48% since 1970. Yet it is the younger singles who are really choosing to live alone these days. The number of those under 25 years old living alone has tripled since 1970, and those 25 to 34 years old, quadrupled.

AUGUST, 1983

LAST MONTH							
S	**M**	**T**	**W**	**T**	**F**	**S**	
	1	2	3	4	5	6	
7	8	9	10	11	12	13	
14	15	16	17	18	19	20	
21	22	23	24	25	26	27	
28	29	30	31				

LAST MONTH

July 1983
S M T W T F S
1 2
3 4 5 6 7 8 9
10 11 12 13 14 15 16
17 18 19 20 21 22 23
24 25 26 27 28 29 30
31

NEXT MONTH

September 1983
S M T W T F S
1 2 3
4 5 6 7 8 9 10
11 12 13 14 15 16 17
18 19 20 21 22 23 24
25 26 27 28 29 30

SUNDAY
219/146
7

Washington Park Concert
parke and ride with
Phil + Lois   7 pm

MONDAY
220/145
8
● NEW MOON

TUESDAY
221/144
9

Volunteer at
Amer Red Cross

WEDNESDAY
222/143
10

THURSDAY
223/142
11

Y- coed
volleyball
game at
noon

FRIDAY
224/141
12

Craft Club — check it out
with Pat

SATURDAY
225/140
13

Flake Out - Shop - washing
AUG. 7 TO 13, 1983

2
INVOLVEMENT AND INFORMATION

GETTING INVOLVED

In our area there are clubs, organizations, and institutions for nearly every conceivable interest, activity, and concern. Whatever turns you on—target shooting, raising roses, dancing, art, western history, listening to jazz, or conservation—there is a group or institution that puts out the welcome mat. And new groups are constantly forming.

Satisfactions mount as you pursue a new or old interest through groups and organizations. Sharing in their purposes and activities enhances the fun and chances for personal accomplishment.

Developing good relationships is partly a matter of finding groups or organizations with which you feel comfortable. Groups and their events encourage those with similar interests, enjoyments, and concerns to find one another. Through them you can find good companions, develop friendships, and perhaps create more intimate attachments.

"Do whatever activities you enjoy—new people are usually the by-product," advises a 34-year-old woman. "I always meet people easiest when I am not there specifically to meet people." Then, "I am relaxed, know that I will have no disappointment about going home alone, and am without expectation that I surely will meet someone special."

If you are convinced about getting involved, or already know how different organizations work, skip the next section. Otherwise, read on.

Your first contact with a new group or activity may be tentative. Or, fueled by well-developed interest, you may rocket into this experience. However done, the pleasure from connecting is yours alone.

Meeting on common ground and sharing in something mutually satisfying: these lead to feeling genuinely involved. Socializing naturally follows, for good relations flourish best among people who feel comfortable together. And for some, busy involvement in a group and its activities helps them feel a sense of community.

Ideally, your presence at an event is not just contrived for social contact. The fact that you are *there*, rather than somewhere else, displays independence and declares your interests. If you are sincerely and enthusiastically engaging in an activity, chances are that you will get along well with the others, who are there for the same reason.

Indeed, "the more activities you pursue, the more well-rounded a person you become," and this creates "a kind of person who other people will want to share time with," one single woman discovered. Involvement in "groups and clubs where I live and work" is the best way a 31-year-old says she found new friends. "I foster the friendship by joining in dinner parties, movies, shopping, etc."

Local groups usually afford friendly and relaxed settings. Visitors typically need only say "hello" before others begin drawing them in. People readily introduce themselves to first-timers. Even if you initially know nobody, you soon will.

One visit is rarely enough. It usually takes two or three times to judge whether the organization or activity is for you. Phone or write ahead to verify meeting places and times, as both may change. Feeling shy? Go first with a friend.

As you begin exploring, you will find great diversity. Some local groups function year-round; some, seasonally. They may focus on one, several, or many activities or may switch around between them. They have anywhere from five to 6,000 members. Their public functions may draw small numbers or big crowds. Groups may be heavily single, heavily paired, or a mix of the two. Children may be absent or present. Some groups require an obvious skill—or at least a willingness to learn it. For others (especially those that spend a lot of time socializing), interest alone is sufficient. And, in every case, participating is more fun than just watching.

Who takes part in local groups? It depends. Some attract mainly people of similar education, income, age, or sex. More men than women, for example, typically attend race car events or belong to flying clubs. If you went to a meeting of the **League of Women Voters** (see chapter 3), you would meet mostly women—although males belong.

Other groups represent a real diversity in age, background, or even interests. That diversity can be very enriching. "Just because you see someone who looks like your parents in a group," cautions a 25-year-old woman, "don't avoid it." You share an interest with them which might foster close, even family-like friendships.

Clubs sometimes sponsor joint events, broadening your connections and experiences. Affiliates of national organizations bring members in touch with people elsewhere, especially if you become—as is often easy—an officer.

Organizations may be intimately involved in their communities, thus involving you. Here, then, are additional chances for personal growth.

And, of course, at any time you may walk away—alone or with another—from any of them.

A plug for volunteering. Volunteering is a strong local and American tradition. For a little investment of time (you *can* find the time), you will reap grand rewards. Volunteer groups and institutions add purpose, structure, vitality, and diversity to our communities. Through volunteering you contribute in turn both to your community and personal satisfaction. If you like the stability and continuity of established things, institutional ties may also be for you.

So build on your concern for animals or the arts, your interest in science, hobbies or sports, your commitments to issues by helping the appropriate volunteer organization. How you use them, what you give or take from them, and what it costs you—that's pretty much up to you.

A 25-year-old woman who wanted to learn radio skills volunteered at **KBOO-FM**, 205 SE Eighth, Portland (231-8032). She reports that this community radio station is run largely by singles between 25 and 40 years old. Friendships quickly grew with those sharing her passion for music. KBOO, incidentally, has money-raising bashes involving music, dancing, drink, and food. Such public events (see chapter 6) are good times to become acquainted with organizations before volunteering.

If you attended a college at least two years, think about joining the local alumni organization. Some are very large. They contribute to their colleges and, through their fellowship and events, to camaraderie.

A 33-year-old woman tells of helping **SOAR** (see chapter 7), which taught her rafting so she could aid disabled persons it takes on excursions. "It is as good a deal for the able-bodied as for a disabled individual because you meet people, have fun, and do things you never thought you would do. The helping part wasn't that big a deal."

I regularly encounter **Oregon Historical Society** (see chapter 6) volunteers. Energetic and knowledgeable, they make invaluable contributions to it. They clearly enjoy spending hours or days among those who share their enthusiasm for Oregon and history. Many comment that they learn something new each time they volunteer.

There are many hundreds of local organizations that depend on volunteers. Some are very big and have paid staffs, such as **The Portland Rose Festival Association**, 1 SW Columbia, Portland (227-2681). Members have a real blowout at Rose Festival time.

Others are small and chummy. In neighborhood associations, you quickly acquire responsibility and get to know neighborhood activists and city officials. What the associations accomplish will be apparent where you live. Check civic calendars in newspapers for neighborhood meeting times and places. Or locate Portland's through the **Office of Neighborhood Associations**, 1220 SW Fifth, Portland (248-5419).

Volunteer Bureau of Greater Portland, 718 W. Burnside, Portland (222-1355) and **Vancouver Volunteer Bu-**

reau, 1703 Main, Vancouver (1-206-694-6577) will match your interests and skills with public and private nonprofit agencies that need volunteers or board members.

KEEPING INFORMED

Anyone can locate almost any group or event in the metropolitan region by knowing a few sources and developing a few mild habits.

- Consult published sources, normally in public libraries. *The Yellow Pages* lists many "Associations," "Clubs," and "Fraternal Organizations." *The Portland Book*, though slightly outdated, includes 540 "Organizations" and 162 "Trade and Professional Associations." Still other groups appear under various headings in *The Portland Women's Yellow Pages*—some are coed—and in *The Portland Guidebook*. The two-volume *Encyclopedia of Associations* describes 16,519 national organizations; their main offices will furnish local contacts. For clubs or associations in places smaller than Portland, check with their Portland chapter.

- Talk about your interests; let people know that you want to hear about certain types of activities or organizations.

- Ask public agencies. For instance, maybe you'd like to learn about fishing groups. Call the **Oregon Department of Fish and Wildlife** (in Portland 299-5403). It will provide contacts for many sporting clubs—bow hunting, rod and gun, fishing and rifle, and pistol groups, for instance. Then call 229-5222 for its recorded information on current wildlife, hunting, and fishing events and regulations in Oregon. To dig up this kind of information, the telephone information service of your public library is a good place to start. At the very least, it can help you find the right agency. The **Multnomah County Library** (223-7201) has a large file of local organizations.

- Keep your eyes open in places associated with your interests. Check bulletin boards, posters, announcements, and literature left there for the taking. Get on mailing lists of groups you like. Their newsletters are frequently excellent for telling you about forthcoming events and similar groups. Go a step further. If an institution is associated with your interests, tap the staff's knowledge. For instance, the public relations department of **Oregon School of Arts and Crafts**, 8245 SW Barnes Rd., Portland (297-5544) will tell you whom to contact for hobby groups and clubs in fields it teaches: ceramics; fibers and textiles; metals; drawing; jewelry design; book crafts; calligraphy; photography; printmaking; and woodworking.

■ Use the mass media for their "billboards" and articles about groups and events. Newspapers print one or more calendars of events each week. *Fresh Weekly*, from *Willamette Week*, and the Friday *Oregonian* are jam-packed with listings, descriptions, ads, and reviews. Sometimes, feature articles are accompanied by names of organizations, as in the *Willamette Week* listing of ten sailing clubs active year-round in the Portland region as of February 1, 1983.

Willamette Week occasionally runs what it terms The List, in two parts. One gives organizations related to the arts and entertainment; the second lists other groups, with a bent toward political, anti-nuclear, environmental, and social service organizations.

The Monday *Daily Journal of Commerce* lists meetings, classes, workshops, and seminars of interest to the business community. Upcoming meetings or business-oriented groups appear in the Monday *Oregonian*. Neighborhood newspapers describe neighborhood groups and events. Also see *The Downtowner*'s calendar. Late each October on Sunday *The Columbian* prints a special section depicting "Clubs and Organizations," mainly in Clark County.

Radio does a slightly better job than television for daily calendars. KBOO-FM broadcasts "Community Calendars" several times daily. KOAP-FM has several arts calendars daily. Many other local stations scatter announcements of events and public meetings through the broadcast day. Radio outside Portland proper seems to announce hometown events more frequently and extensively than do Portland stations, a local broadcaster says.

Monthly publications are also good sources. See the statewide calendar in *Oregon Magazine*. *Multnomah Monthly Magazine* and *Portland*, published by the Chamber of Commerce, also have calendars. *Transformation Times* has new-age, personal growth, and holistic health events and organizations. *The Alliance*, published by the Alliance for Social Change, prints a calendar of events and descriptions of local organizations devoted to social change.

If you ask monthly at the desk of the **Greater Portland Convention and Visitors Association**, 26 SW Salmon, Portland, for its free events calendar—or subscribe to it—you can see where the media learns about many present and forthcoming happenings.

OCTOBER, 1983

LAST MONTH

September 1983
S M T W T F S
1 2 3
4 5 6 7 8 9 10
11 12 13 14 15 16 17
18 19 20 21 22 23 24
25 26 27 28 29 30

NEXT MONTH

November 1983
S M T W T F S
1 2 3 4 5
6 7 8 9 10 11 12
13 14 15 16 17 18 19
20 21 22 23 24 25 26
27 28 29 30

SUNDAY
275/090
2

Jazz Society Concert 7:30

MONDAY
276/089
3

Toastmaster's Club Meeting

TUESDAY
277/088
4

Finish Sets for Play

WEDNESDAY
278/087
5

Neighborhood Assn meeting. Bring up tree limb problem 7:00

THURSDAY
279/086
6
● NEW MOON

FRIDAY
280/085
7

SATURDAY
281/084
8

Cast Party!

OCT. 2 TO 8, 1983

3

GENERAL GROUPS AND EVENTS

BUSINESS AND PROFESSIONAL

Each profession, business, and trade seems to have a dues-paying association. Many welcome the general public at meetings and activities. For both members and visitors, they offer chances to socialize casually.

I describe the tiniest number of possibilities. In your own field, you probably already know the groups. For other fields, you can check *The Portland Book*, which found 162 associations in 1979.

Many associations are heavily male or female. One 34-year-old business person enjoys "Business After Hours" partly because these no-host cocktail parties in Portland introduce her to lots of business*men*. You can find times, locations, and costs in the weekly bulletins published by the Portland Chamber of Commerce.

Portland Chamber of Commerce, 824 SW Fifth, Portland (228-9411) and **Chamber of Commerce of Greater Vancouver**, 510 W. Mill Plain Blvd., Vancouver (1-206-694-2588), are two of the many Chambers listed in area phone books. Portland's Chamber claims 3,600 member companies and 6,000 active volunteers. All the Chambers represent and study local growth, industry, and business. Members accomplish much of their work in committees.

American Business Women's Association, 15425 NE Holladay, Portland (227-3223) also has several Vancouver-area chapters. Call them at 1-206-573-6102, 1-206-573-3399, 1-206-254-6237, 1-206-254-9282, or 1-206-574-0625. All female, the Association means to speed the professional, educational, cultural, and social advancement of women in business. Monthly meetings feature speakers.

Institute for Managerial and Professional Women, PO Box 1747, Portland 97207 (226-7701) has a largely female membership. It provides career clarification, managerial and professional skills, and networking resources. The Institute holds workshops and training conferences, monthly breakfast forums, and a monthly training program.

CIVIC AND SERVICE

Civic and service organizations exist to provide service to their communities and, in the process, personal development for their members. They can also be terrific places to meet people. Only a sampling is possible here.

American Association of University Women, 4050 SE Gladstone, Rm. 16, Portland (777-7005) will put you in touch with chapters in Beaverton, Gladstone, Lake Oswego, Milwaukie, Oregon City, and Tigard. For Vancouver, call 1-206-693-8963. Open to women graduates of accredited colleges and universities, AAUW sponsors study action projects, workshops, self-growth groups, conferences, fellowships, and publications.

International Toastmaster has 64 clubs in the Portland area. The Portland Chamber of Commerce (228-9411) can help you locate one that is convenient for you. Six Vancouver-area Toastmaster clubs are listed in "Clubs and Organizations," a Sunday supplement to *The Columbian* published each late October. The Toastmasters' goal is self-improvement, particularly through improved communication. Members make frequent speeches and conduct meetings to sharpen organizational and leadership skills and inspire self-confidence; assessments follow. Clubs are coeducational and limited to 40 persons; most meet weekly. One is limited to singles: Servetus' Toastmaster Club, which meets at Manning Cafeteria in Portland's Lloyd Center (Holly, 644-4563).

International Toastmistress has 27 clubs in the Portland area. In Oregon, contact Marjorie at 646-8814 to locate one that is convenient for you; for those in the Vancouver area, contact Carmen at 1-206-699-4242 w. Men and women members practice organizational and leadership skills by frequent speechmaking in the clubs. "Any individual who seeks self-improvement and personal enrichment is a potential Toastmistress," the clubs proclaim. Clubs are limited to 30 members and often meet weekly. A local Toastmistress official stresses that it does things differently from Toastmasters clubs.

Jaycees, 824 SW Fifth, Portland (227-5656) also furnishes contacts for Jaycees in Gresham, Canby, Milwaukie, Oregon City, Beaverton, Gladstone, and Troutdale. For Vancouver, contact Martin, 3714 NE 65th, Vancouver (1-206-695-4964). For Camas-Washougal, contact Jim, 138 Sixth, Washougal (1-206-835-3113). Jaycees offer men—only the Portland chapter is coeducational—opportunities to develop their talents and skills through participation in community service projects. Typical ones might deal with pollution, drugs, crime, health, safety, energy, and the environment. Portland Jaycees are for those from 18 to 36 years old; other chapters vary the top age.

Jayceetees (or **Lady Jaycees**), c/o its state office, PO Box 13111, Salem 97309 (1-378-7041) provides contacts for its chapters in Gresham, Beaverton-Tigard, Hillsboro, East Portland, Damascus-Boring, and elsewhere. For Vancouver, contact Theresa, 1602 Ash, Vancouver (1-206-695-6945). Lady Jaycees feature leadership training and civic involvement for women between 18 and 36 years old or 21 to 40 in Vancouver. Their aims are similar to the Jaycees, whom they join in community projects.

National Council of Jewish Women, 3030 SW Second, Portland (222-5006) has 700 members, mainly Jewish women, although men and non-Jews belong, too. It meets quarterly. The Portland Section devotes itself to education, community service, and social action. Its priorities are aging, children and youth, Israel, Jewish life, and women's issues. The group also sponsors tours and local workshops, projects, and programs. It runs a thrift shop.

POLITICAL

Exploit your political interests. Political campaigns are known for their social, not just political, action. You can do a little or a lot. Campaign work can be drudgery and tiring, even for the convinced. But the work does have an end, and you *do* meet loads of people, singles especially. Close quarters over weeks guarantee real knowledge of one another.

Why wait for campaigns? Political parties have meetings and activities between campaigns. Every county has its Democratic and Republican clubs. Caucuses exist within and coalitions exist between parties. Smaller political parties have year-round schedules.

Political action groups are everywhere. They typically lavish responsibility on you quickly. Try working at the grass roots. You will find that individuals who share strong views—normal in these organizations—tend to forge durable bonds.

League of Women Voters, 519 SW Third, Rm. 610, Portland (228-1675) also has chapters in East Multnomah County, 15231 NE Holladay, Portland (252-6060); in East Washington County, 11650 SW Clifford, Beaverton (644-7573); in West Washington County, 1208 Cedar, Forest Grove (357-3004); in West Clackamas County, 3700 Upper Dr., Lake Oswego (636-5468); in Milwaukie-East Clackamas County, 45210 SE Coleman Rd., Portland (668-4314); and in the Vancouver area, 19004 NE 116th, Battle Ground, WA (1-206-687-3942). The League is a big, very active coeducational nonpartisan organization. It furthers informed citizen participation in government through a vast range of activities.

THE ARTS

Scores of arts groups provide creative, disciplined, and enjoyable outlets for anyone's artistic talents and interests. Expect the company of sociable types. "Following my interests in music and dance led to most people I know," reports a 28-year-old man. Performing arts groups are strong on camaraderie.

The groups listed below perform publicly. While they look

like laundry lists, each set below is ripe with worthwhile possibilities. (Also see chapter 6 for arts institutions, such as museums.)

Acting and music groups normally require auditions. To locate auditions, consult the organization or heed newspaper and radio announcements. You might also ask directors of the listed groups to suggest small performing groups or those which perform solely for their own enjoyment. Their members, too, have lots of fun.

THEATER

Community theater, like musical groups, involves committed individuals, many of them single. Lively cast parties are traditional and often attract people from past productions. Those interested in acting must be willing to spend considerable time evenings and perhaps weekends with the same cast. Building sets, selling tickets, and other forms of participation are usually less time consuming.

Encore Players, Columbia Art Center, 400 SW Evergreen Blvd., Vancouver (Jean, 1-206-254-5023).

Firehouse Theatre, 1436 SW Montgomery, Portland (248-4737).

Lake Oswego Community Theatre, Lakewood Center for the Arts, 368 S. State, Lake Oswego (635-3901).

The Old Slocum House Theater Company, 605 Esther, Vancouver.

Peanut Gallery, Clark College Theater Department, Vancouver (1-206-694-6521).

Portland Civic Theatre, 1530 SW Yamhill, Portland (226-3048).

Pub Theater, 1431 NE Broadway, Portland (287-1431).

Sandy Community Players, 38935 Proctor, Sandy (668-7737 or Jim, 661-0219 w).

Theatre Workshop, 511 SE 60th, Portland (235-4551).

Theater in the Grove, 2033 Pacific, Forest Grove (359-5565).

MUSIC

"For anyone who has ever sung, even in the past, singing groups like the Portland Chorale are great ways to sing and also wonderful places for meeting people from a wide background and age range," reports a Portland Chorale officer. Church and synagogue choirs also need good voices.

Brahms Singers, c/o 3800 E. Clark, Vancouver (1-206-296-2101). Serious music.

Choral Arts Ensemble of Portland. Call Eare in Portland at 644-3151. Serious music, some lighter.

Columbia Chamber Singers. Call Eugene in Portland at 760-2749. Serious music, some lighter.

The Francis Street Singers, Community Music Center, 3350 SE Francis, Portland (235-8222). Almost everything.

Mount Hood Community Choir, Mt. Hood Community College Music Department, Gresham (667-7155).

Northwest Repertory Choir. Call in Portland 241-2440. Basically operatic.

Oregon Repertory Singers, PO Box 894, Portland Federal Station (277-3929). Serious music.

Oregon Vocal Arts Ensemble. Call in Portland 646-3233. Mainly serious.

Portland Chorale. Call Wilbur in Gresham at 255-9026 h or 255-9877 w. Almost everything.

Portland Community College Community Choir. Call in Portland (645-4461, ext. 220). Almost everything.

Portland Gay Men's Chorus, PO Box 3223, Portland 97208 (287-5966). Almost everything.

Portland State University Choir and **Portland State University Chamber Choir**. Call Bruce in Portland at 229-3063. Open to auditors and senior citizens. Mainly serious.

Portland Symphonic Choir, 510 SW Fifth, Portland (233-1217). The big civic choral group. Major serious works.

Studio Lyric Theater, 1522 SE Tacoma, Portland (231-9582). Gilbert and Sullivan plus Broadway and revue-type works.

֎

The following instrumental groups usually play wide repertoires:

Beaverton Community Band. Call Keith in Beaverton at 639-4477.

Cabin Fever Moonshine Band, Clackamas Community College (657-8400, ext. 434). Country, folk, and bluegrass music.

Marylhurst Symphony Orchestra, Marylhurst College for Lifelong Learning, Marylhurst (636-8141 or 224-5828).

Mittleman Jewish Community Center Orchestra. Call Albert in Portland at 649-8421.

Mount Hood Community Orchestra and **Mount Hood Community Band**, Mt. Hood Community College Music Department (667-7155).

Pacific University Community Orchestra, Forest Grove (Kenneth Combs, 357-6151).

Palatine Hill Symphony Orchestra. Call Jerry Luedders in Portland at 244-6161, ext. 297.

Portland Chamber Orchestra. Call Paul in Portland at 244-6207.

Portland Community College Community Band and **Portland Community College Orchestra**. Call in Portland 645-4461, ext. 220.

University of Portland Community Orchestra, Music Department (283-7319).

Vancouver Symphonette and **Westwinds Community Band**, c/o 860 S. Friedel Ave., Vancouver (1-206-694-1976).

❧

Among the many musical groups promoting live music and encouraging members to make music together are the following:

Jazz Society of Oregon, PO Box 968, Portland 97207 (254-6348 or 363-0372) promotes a wide range of jazz during picnics, concerts, and other events. Its Jazz Weekend at the Inn at Otter Crest, though expensive, is a "dynamite place to meet other single people," including the musicians, reports a 43-year-old man.

Oregon Bluegrass Association, PO Box 1115, Portland 97207, is a 550-member club, embracing all ages, which sponsors concerts and festivals of bluegrass and closely related music. It meets the second Sunday each month. About 30% of the membership is single.

Oregon City Traditional Jazz Society, PO Box 214, Oregon City 97045 (Carolyn in Portland 661-2539 mornings or Doris in Oregon City 254-4195) promotes traditional and Dixieland jazz and ragtime. It has jazz and dancing, parties, or picnics every weekend. Children are welcome. Anyone may play between musicians' sets. It switches events between Oregon City, Portland, and elsewhere.

Portland Family Sing, 2923 NE 18th, Portland (282-9222) has informal singing the third Sunday evening each month. Bring only your love of singing plus instruments, music books, and song sheets.

Portland Folklore Society, c/o 5256 NE 47th, Portland (281-7475) promotes folk music, folk dance, and folk arts. It meets the third Sunday evening each month, except summers, for a potluck-meeting. PFS sponsors concerts, folk singing groups, occasional parties, and other events. (For its first and third Thursday folk music concerts at the Metropolitan Learning Center in Portland, see chapter 6.) About 80 belong, mostly single.

Portland Recorder Society, c/o Augustana Lutheran Church, 2710 NE 17th, Portland (288-6174) has small and large recorder and "buzzie" ensemble playing at all expertise levels each second Friday evening monthly.

LITERARY

Great Books Discussion Groups exist at the downtown Multnomah County Library (contact Mrs. Scarl in Portland at 239-9990) and in private homes. Participants read one or two classic works each month, and a moderator runs two-hour discussions. Books are bought in sets or borrowed. Anyone may form new Great Books Discussion Groups.

If you like poetry or want to read your own, head down to the **Mediterranean Tavern**, 1650 W. Burnside, Portland (222-1507) on Wednesday evenings and to **Cafe Oasis**, 1616 NW 23rd, Portland (222-5253) on Tuesday evenings. **Chocolate Moose**, 211 SW Ankeny, Portland (222-5753) hosts open poetry readings on first and third Sunday evenings each month. Local women poets read at the **Northwest Artists' Workshop**, 522 NW 12th, Portland (777-0406) on second Thursday evenings each month. Invited poets and fiction writers read at the **Blackfish Gallery**, 325 NW Sixth, Portland (775-4582) on the third Tuesday evening each month. Local colleges also have poetry readings.

OUTDOORS

SKIING

Skiing is a major regional pleasure and can be highly social. Individuals meet readily in nearby ski lodges and on ski slopes. Some elect to "ski the lodge" rather than the slopes. Many like the sociability (and lower group rates) of ski clubs listed below.

Bergfreunde Ski Club, PO Box 321, Portland 97207 or Marralenne, 10573 SW Murdock, Tigard (638-0222 h, 224-3525 w) promotes recreational skiing and sports. The club has weeklong and weekend ski trips, weekly volleyball, rafting, sailing and camping trips, ski racing teams, ski exercise classes, waterskiing, weekly tennis matches, a golf tournament, coed softball teams, and a monthly party. It meets monthly. Some 450 belong, 40% of whom are under 30 years old. The membership is 90% single. Nonmembers pay extra and may attend most events.

Edge Set Ski Club, 12260 SW Faircrest, Portland (646-5292) is open to all over 21 years old. It schedules weekend skiing at Mt. Bachelor every third weekend; until five days before trips, members have priority. Forty-five usually ski, ranging in age from 26 to 50, with most between 32 and 42. The club is 55% single.

Mount Hood Community College Ski Club, c/o College Center, 2600 SE Stark, Gresham (667-7252) includes nonstudents among its 63 members. It has weekend trips to Mt. Hood, longer ski trips elsewhere, and social events, some in the off-season. Nonmembers may join some of their skiing activities.

Oregon Nordic Club, 22 SW A Ave., Lake Oswego (636-4061) promotes cross-country skiing and other sports, such as hiking. It, too, has social events. Members are mostly between 25 and 35 years old, although older persons belong.

Plaza Ski Club, PO Box 4500-12, Portland 97208 (771-

0047) is for all over 21 years old, including non-skiers. Weekend and longer ski trips are for members only, but nonskiers may join its racquetball, picnics, camping, water skiing, rafting, ski classes, and parties. About 90% of the 300 members are single, and most are between 25 and 35 years old.

Schnee Vogeli Ski Club, PO Box 42383, Portland 97342 (Gene, 224-9700) is an all-male, invitation-only club with several well-attended public events. The 120-member club sponsors two popular weekend races, a slalom, a snow dance at Government Camp, and a used equipment sale.

Skiyente Ski Club, PO Box 5132, Portland 97209, is for women over 21 years old, preferably skiers. Its 50 members meet twice monthly during ski season. They sponsor ski and fun races, a dance at Mt. Hood, and a dinner. Men are invited to some functions. Members range from 21 to 65, with most between 25 and 40 years old; 80% are single.

Ski-Tek, PO Box 500 MS 50/157, Beaverton 97007 (Schnowe phone 641-1071) is the largest of the ski clubs, with some 500 members over 18 years old. It has weekend ski trips to Bend, a weekly trip elsewhere, Friday night buses, parties at Timberline Lodge, ski classes, and a spring beach party. Most members are in their twenties and early thirties; 80% are single.

Union Pacific Ski Club, PO Box 8979, Portland 97208 (Harold, 249-2360 w) is composed of singles (80%) and couples from different companies. It skis regularly. Only members may attend its week-long ski trips. Offseason, the club has campouts, raft trips, a baseball game, barbecues, and parties. Of its more than 70 members from 21 to 41 years old, most are between 27 and 34 years old.

ON THE WATER

Lower Columbia Canoe Club, PO Box 40210, Portland 97240, has over 200 members, about 20% of them single. It has canoe trips weekly from March through October, runs clinics, including whitewater, and promotes safe and enjoyable waterway use. The club meets the second Saturday each month for a potluck and program. Members come from a wide age range, with most between 21 and 50 years old.

Northwest Rafters Association, PO Box 19008, Portland

97219 (Al, 246-0386) has 200 members participating in its whitewater rafting and float trips at least twice monthly on local rivers. The club is interested in preservation and conservation and in educating members and the public about rafting. Members are from 20 to 70, with most between 25 and 45 years old.

Oregon Kayak and Canoe Club, PO Box 692, Portland 97207, has whitewater trips from March through November, a race, and members who schedule kayaking classes. About 100 belong, mostly from 21 to 50 years old.

Vancouver Lake Sailing Club, 7110 NW 25th, Vancouver (1-206-693-9752) has a racing schedule and teaches sailing.

Willamette Sailing Club, 6336 SW Beaver, Portland (246-9140) mainly has a family membership. It has active racing and social schedules and teaches sailing.

WILDERNESS AND WILDLIFE

Association of Northwest Steelheaders, 7225 SE 22nd Pl., Portland (232-0517) also has chapters on the Sandy River (Doug, 1619 SE Knarr Ct., Troutdale 666-4165) and two in Washington County (14815 SE Hall Blvd., Tigard and PO Box 131, Beaverton 97005). For Clark County, contact Chuck Voss, Association of Northwest Steelheaders, PO Box Q, Woodland, WA 98674 (1-206-225-6284). Members of this club share an interest in steelhead and salmon fishing. They run fishing clinics, discuss fishing, work on conservation legislation, fish and party together.

Mazamas, 909 NW 19th, Portland (227-2345) is a nationally famous hiking and climbing club. Members must have climbed to the summit of a glaciated mountain by foot. The club holds climbing classes to qualify new members and to improve climbing skills. Whitewater rafting classes are available in spring to members and nonmembers. Members and a few specially guided students explore alpine regions of the Pacific Northwest and elsewhere. The club sponsors weekend trail hikes, rafting trips, outings for climbers and families, weekly summer picnics, and weekly evening programs. Its 2,800 members, many single, range from 14 to 80 years old; most are in their thirties. Nonmembers pay higher participation fees.

Oregon Bass and Panfish Club, PO Box 1021, Portland 97207 (282-2852) has 600 members of all ages interested in warm-water fishing. The fourth Thursday each month (sometimes bimonthly) it meets to learn about or go to good fishing spots. It runs how to and where to fish clinics, sponsors an equipment sale, and works to improve fish habitats.

Oregon Duck Hunters Association, 4533 NE 35th Pl., Portland (281-9509) has 450 members, mostly male, interested in safe hunting practices and habitat conservation in Oregon and Canada. Meeting the second Wednesday each month, the club also runs hunter clinics, information nights, fundraising and social events, and engages in lobbying.

Portland Audubon Association, 5151 NW Cornell Rd., Portland (292-6855) also has subchapters in the eastern and southern parts of the metropolitan area. For Vancouver, contact Vancouver Audubon Society, c/o CLP, 4312 NE 40th (1-206-695-2777). Audubon chapters study and protect wildlife. The Portland chapter meets twice monthly, except summers, for programs on natural history and conservation issues. It sponsors wildlife films, a rare bird sighting recorded message, classes, field trips, and educational and wildlife rehabilitation programs and sanctuaries. About half those on its educational hikes are single. The 3,300-member Portland chapter draws from all ages. Events are public.

Portland Gay Hiking Club, c/o Andy, 131 SE 24th, Apt. D, Portland, welcomes gay men and lesbians to its day hikes, backpacking trips, rafting, mountaineering, bicycling, cross-country skiing, potlucks, and picnics. Most participating are between 25 and 35 years old.

Ptarmigans Mountaineering Club, PO Box 1821, Vancouver 98668 (1-206-695-5510) arranges mountain, ice and rock climbing, skiing, canoeing, rafting, bicycling, hiking, and backpacking trips, some outside Oregon and Washington. There are usually two activities each weekend; if there is room, non-members with proper skills may attend outings. The 100-member club meets monthly and sponsors an outdoor school in May. Members are between 16 and 60 years old. The climbers are mostly under 40 years old; the canoers, bicyclers, and hikers, all ages.

Sierra Club, 2637 Water St., Portland (outing tape 224-1538 or Bruce, 244-0885) strives to conserve and preserve the natural environment. It has weekend outings to wilderness areas, day hikes, snowshoe hikes, cross-country skiing, and similar events. This region-wide chapter also devotes attention to lobbying, litigation, and educational work. More than 100 gather weekly for work sessions-potlucks, committee meetings, or special events. Members range from their twenties into their fifties, with most in their thirties. About half of the 2,700 members are single. Nonmembers may attend most events.

Upwards Trails, 20606 NE Interlachen Ln., Troutdale (667-3405) is a doctrinally based outreach to evangelical Christian singles and eventually wants to be family-oriented. The club teaches wilderness behavior. It has hiking, backpacking, climbing, rafting, cross-country and downhill skiing, snowshoeing, winter camping, a yearly winter snow retreat, and tours. The club bans rock music, cards, alcohol, and tobacco. There are from 15 to 30 members, ranging in age from 22 to 50 years old, with most in their early thirties. Retreats attract from 60 to 80 people.

Izaak Walton League, 13135 NE Brazee, Portland (Chuck, 253-8135); and for Air Force-Lewis and Clark, Oregon City, and Washington County chapters, contact Glen, 7365 SW 82nd, Portland (246-9622). The League works to preserve natural resources and wildlife, to increase outdoor recreation opportunities, and to encourage conservation legislation. The Portland chapter has 150 members between ages 30 and 70; other chapters are smaller. Portland's has weekly programs plus Friday lunch meetings with speakers.

BICYCLING

Portland Wheelman Club, PO Box 40753, Portland 97240 has 350 members and sponsors weekend rides of from 15 to 200 miles. So it is for the experienced rider, not the beginner.

Rose City Wheelmen, 2346 NE 40th, Portland (Michael, 281-2250) sponsors long bicycle rides, a 200-mile bicycle tour of the Columbia Gorge, bike races, including one during Portland Rose Festival time, and cross-country skiing. Fifteen to 20 experienced riders belong. About 20% are single.

OTHER SPORTS AND HOBBIES

One Friday in September *The Oregonian* Leisure Section listed upcoming events held by the Oregon Beaver Bottle Club, Class-E Hooking Artists, Northwest Vintage Radio Society, and Northwest Rafters Association. A classic and antique car show was mentioned. Several craft shows—good places to learn of craft clubs—were scheduled. A biweekly Great Books Discussion Club would begin midweek. Columns and announcements elsewhere in the paper alerted readers to still more hobby and sports groups and events. And that was only a small sample of attractions in the metropolitan area in a typical week.

You can attend such events as a browser, with nothing much in mind, or use them to gauge personal interest, or join right in. (For disabled persons, see the special opportunities in chapter 8.)

Hobby and sports groups require some skill, but maybe not a lot. If you become an active participant, your skills will improve.

Pride of purpose and accomplishment—real joy—mark many of these groups. Watch the mutual enjoyment, enthusiasm, and other good things happening on softball and bowling teams and in pickup and team volleyball or basketball games in parks and recreation centers, bowling alleys, Y's, community centers, and Community Schools' gyms.

Afterward, teammates may relax comfortably in nearby bars and restaurants. A 32-year-old woman on a women's soccer team of the Portland Parks and Recreation Bureau happily discovered that it partied with male soccer teams.

Twelve Portland Community Schools have open basketball times, 13 have open, mainly coeducational, volleyball times, and **Binnsmead**, 2225 SE 87th, Portland (771-0121), among them, has open badminton. Community Schools issues a free quarterly catalog, which is also included in the free quarterly Portland Parks catalog.

There's no better way to get to know your neighbors or workmates than to play on a team with them. Find out about existing teams or list yours for league play with **Portland Parks and Recreation Bureau** (769-5150) or the comparable community agency. Unions, companies, and churches provide the wherewithal for all sorts of sports and hobby groups.

Running events are really solo activities. The annual **Cascade Runoff** does arrange a no-host picnic afterward. (The thousands of volunteer hours which make it and other big events possible provide abundant occasions to meet fellow volunteers.) **Oregon Road Runners**, PO Box D, Beaverton, has a tape (223-7867) on scheduled running events.

Skaters visit with one another in **Laurelhurst Park**, where skates are rented summer weekends, at **Mt. Scott Community Center**'s small rink, 5530 SE 72nd Portland (774-2215), and at commercial rinks. At roller and ice skating rinks, "people help each other up and meet—or crash into others" and meet, a 27-year-old male skater observes.

Bowling may begin as a solitary activity, then gather in nearby people. Experienced bowlers and lane employees gladly give pointers to the less expert. Some bowling alleys offer child care. If you're interested in playing on a team, one of the following can help you identify an appropriate one:

Portland Bowling Association in Portland at 239-7163 (for men).

Greater Portland Women's Bowling Association in Portland at 239-7160.

Clark County Women's Bowling Association in Vancouver at 1-206-693-8364.

Suppose you have less active interests? Continue reading to the end of this section, then.

Camera clubs usually have 20 to 45 members, mostly in their forties and fifties. Clubs meet regularly and usually conduct classes and workshops. (Younger singles are using darkrooms at community colleges and commercial enterprises, according to a 27-year-old man.) Here are a few clubs:

Portland Photographic Society, c/o Walton, 12705 SE River Rd., Portland (654-5581) has 90 members and meets twice a month. It has slide and print critiques and judging, seminars, and bus tours to photogenic Pacific Northwest spots.

Film Pack Camera Club, PO Box 2093, Vancouver 98661 (Delmar, 1-206-695-4088 or Emil, 1-206-695-5270) has weekly competitions, field trips, and social events.

Forest Grove Camera Club, PO Box 132, Forest Grove 97116 is similar and also has public exhibitions, lectures, and demonstrations. It meets weekly September through May.

Oregon Camera Club, PO Box 230221, Portland 97223 (244-1587) has print and slide judging and public exhibits. Some nights it uses models. There are no meetings in summer.

Pacific Color Printers, 4133 SE 74th, Portland (774-2025 or Ted, 244-1587) focuses on demonstrations and talks and on judging members' entries of color slides. There are no meetings in July and August.

Singles are well-represented at meetings, open houses, and the monthly stamp fair of the **Oregon Stamp Society**, 4828 NE 33rd, Portland (949-9047 or 282-2706). For the **Fort Vancouver Stamp Club**, contact John, PO Box 154, Vancouver 98666 (1-206-693-1841).

On most Sunday afternoons, you may play a rated game under tournament conditions with civilized time controls at the **Portland Chess Club**, 2806 SE Powell (232-7027).

Card playing is an immensely popular pastime. Bridge and pinochle games are regular features at several Portland community centers. Or you can try one of the Portland bridge centers, which also teach bridge, listed in *The Yellow Pages*. Or contact Mrs. H.E.M., **American Contract Bridge League**, 3301 G St., Vancouver, or Sue, **Vancouver Duplicate Bridge Club**, 611 Umatilla Way, Vancouver (1-206-694-0646).

Columbia Gorge Model Railroading Club, 2505 N. Vancouver, Portland (288-7246) is building a vastly enlarged Columbia River model railroad network in its clubhouse. Members sporting railroad duds and patches will then conduct spectacular public shows once again. Members come from a wide background.

OTHER GROUPS

All-Ireland Cultural Society, PO Box 3411, Portland 97208 (281-8751) is an active ethnic organization. The 270-member Society sponsors Irish cultural events and promotes Irish traditions through dancing, picnics, parties, classes, and other activities. Interest in things Irish qualifies anyone for membership. Many singles belong, and members span a wide age range.

Association for Humanistic Psychology (in Portland, call Paul, 234-6954 or Evan, 245-4869) explores, creates, and shares in humanistic unfolding and living. It meets regularly for networking, social and educational activities, and mutual support of positive human interaction.

El Círculo Español (in Portland, call Paul, 231-6400 w) promotes Spanish culture and language. It has lunchtime cultural and educational programs in downtown Portland twice monthly.

Le Circle Francais (in Portland, call 654-6208) promotes French culture and language. It has lunchtime cultural and educational programs in downtown Portland twice monthly.

Oregon MENSA—The High IQ Society, PO Box 4502, Portland 97208 (223-4502) or 10511 SE Crystal Lane, Milwaukie (Anne, 653-2842), or in Vancouver, call 1-206-699-5279. MENSA stresses contact between intelligent people. It meets monthly and has smaller study and special-interest groups and informal social gatherings. Members are from many ages and backgrounds. Scoring in the top 2% of an IQ test is required for membership.

Society for Creative Anachronism, c/o Peter, 1232 SW Jefferson, Portland (228-3326 afternoons) and for the Vancouver chapter, contact either Laurie, 3009 E. McLoughlin, Vancouver (1-206-693-4663) or David, 4045 SE Cora, Portland (774-1812 after 4 p.m.). The club studies all aspects of the Middle Ages and recreates the better ones. Tournaments, revels, classes, demonstrations, and interest-group meetings are devoted to medieval warfare, arts and crafts, food and costumes. While the Society draws all ages, including children, it mainly attracts those interested in history, fantasy, science fiction, and theater. (For its weekly medieval and renaissance dances in Vancouver, see chapter 5.)

OCTOBER, 1983

LAST MONTH

September						1983
S	M	T	W	T	F	S
					1	2	3
4	5	6	7	8	9	10
11	12	13	14	15	16	17
18	19	20	21	22	23	24
25	26	27	28	29	30	

S	M	T	W	T	F	S
						1
2	3	4	5	6	7	8
9	10	11	12	13	14	15
16	17	18	19	20	21	22
23 30	24 31	25	26	27	28	29

NEXT MONTH

November						1983
S	M	T	W	T	F	S
		1	2	3	4	5
6	7	8	9	10	11	12
13	14	15	16	17	18	19
20	21	22	23	24	25	26
27	28	29	30			

SUNDAY
303/062
30

join brunch with other singles club 11 AM

MONDAY
304/061
31

Halloween

Party with singles club 9:00

TUESDAY
305/060
1

Bowling Night

WEDNESDAY
306/059
2

Jan's birthday — drinks after work

THURSDAY
307/058
3

REST

FRIDAY
308/057
4
● NEW MOON

Evening swim — bring towel 7 pm

SATURDAY
309/056
5

Box Social — Barn dance

OCT. 30 TO NOV. 5, 1983

4
SINGLES GROUPS
AND EVENTS

WHAT SINGLES
ORGANIZATIONS OFFER

Ask yourself a few questions.

Do you enjoy the companionship of single men and women who really understand and support the single's existence?

Do you like being able to go alone comfortably to functions? Especially casual, usually low-cost, and convenient functions? Where acquaintanceships blossom and friendships develop naturally out of shared activities and outlooks? Where, for instance, people often enjoy holidays together?

Do you favor small, intimate gatherings? Where singles are relaxed, responsive, and usually open to one another? Where you are not pressured to pair off?

If you answered "yes," Portland area singles organizations are worth serious consideration. They are run by and for singles. A few try to serve the social and recreational wants of all single people. Others provide companionship for those who share a special interest or characteristic. The majority—in numbers but not necessarily in size—are meant for those of comparable spiritual or religious persuasion who want to share time together.

None deserve the "meat market" or "body exchange" reputation which keep some singles from ever trying them. Indeed, a 36-year-old woman "discovered that I don't need a man/boyfriend/date on weekends to have a social life, thanks to all the single groups! That's been a big relief, and I've stopped dating indiscriminately since then."

Members of these clubs usually try to put newcomers at their ease and draw them into the swing of things. Singles clubs tend to favor get-acquainted sessions. Or you may take off to a sports event, concert, or tour with them. Emphasis is on including, not excluding people. Some clubs frequently participate in joint activities with other singles organizations.

Which one is right for you? Try several types of club functions before deciding. Dissimilar events—and even the same sort of functions—may attract different people from week to week. If unsatisfied, attend again in a few months. These clubs change fast in numbers, personalities, and profiles. *You* may also have changed in the meantime.

Receiving their newsletters or newspapers is essential, as these clubs seldom advertise functions. Their publications are wonderfully newsy, too: complimenting people on birthdays, awards and marriages; remembering past members; sharing information on happenings outside the club.

Watch bulletin boards, newsletters, and ads for new singles groups forming. Classified ads have also brought adventurous singles together to dine or sing, play bridge or volleyball (followed by beers), and for weekly "happy hours" in bars. (See the final chapter.) Check, too, for singles clubs in churches and synagogues.

Organizations not listed in this chapter are in private clubs, in churches publicizing their presence solely to churchgoers, and clubs maintained only by personal invitation. Several supposed singles clubs in the Vancouver area did not reply to my inquiries; they are not included.

Of course, call ahead, as meeting times and locations change.

THE BIG ONES

Servetus for Single Adults, 2005 SE 82nd, No. 6, Portland (774-7337)—for events in Vancouver contact Margueritte in Vancouver at 1-206-695-8707; for those in Camas, contact Lila at 1-206-834-3383—offers one to three functions *daily*. Members get the monthly newsletter and discounts to club events.

(There is a free three-month trial membership.) Nonmembers can attend any event for a modest fee. Or subscribe just to the newsletter if you simply want to know what is happening.

And happening it is. Sundays at Servetus means breakfasts in both west and east Portland (one with Valley Singles, discussed below), dinners, dance classes, hikes, picnics, and drives or visits—with or without children—to events and places nearby.

"We hope you will come" to a get-acquainted coffee held at least one Monday evening a month at its clubhouse, Servetus says. Another group usually meets to play billiards and pool that evening.

Tuesday evening Servetus runs a small, singles-only Toastmaster club for men and women. It meets over dinner in Lloyd Center. (See chapter 3.)

Wednesday mornings Servetus gathers again at Manning Cafeteria in Lloyd Center for a Kaffee Klatch. That evening, it's dancing and cards in the clubhouse.

Golfers tee off on warm Thursdays. Rap sessions or speakers occupy the clubhouse Thursday evenings. Or they go to Servetus' midweek gathering that night at **The Woodshed**, 16015 SE Stark, Portland, for music and dancing.

Pinochle attracts Friday nighters to the clubhouse. Singles from around the region meanwhile attend Servetus' public dances almost every Friday night. (See chapter 5.)

Saturday nights feature potlucks or parties, travel films, hoedown dancing, or game nights at the clubhouse or in members' homes. Or Servetus goes out dancing.

When members are not busy elsewhere, they are off on tours or dropping in for conversation during club office hours.

Fifteen hundred singles believe Servetus valuable enough to take its newspaper. The number of those attending its functions depends on the event. Servetus officers say that the level of physical activity largely determines the age of the crowd; the more sedentary the event, the older those attending. My own impression is that those attending—members or not—mainly are over 40.

Singles Together, 3405 SE Westview, Milwaukie (654-4367) has roughly as many functions as Servetus but not necessarily every day. Weekends, it goes outdoors much more often than Servetus does. It mails 1,200 free bimonthly newsletters. Singles Together depends on volunteers and modest participation fees. Unlike Servetus, it has no established meeting place. Events lure different size crowds. Participants are usually older than 35, according to its leaders. Children are part of some functions.

Sundays bring bowling. "Your score isn't important, so everyone has a good time. Your teenagers are encouraged to bowl with us and your younger ones can come and watch from the viewing area," the newsletter announces.

On Mondays, the club connects with a coed Toastmaster dinner meeting in Lake Oswego (Esther, 636-3154, and see chapter 3 for Toastmasters).

Tuesdays, one group plays cards and games while another goes dancing at the Eagles. (See chapter 5.)

Wednesdays, Singles Together joins Episcopal Singles of Portland (see below) for open and power volleyball games. Afterward, they go out for pizza and beverages.

There are various events on Thursdays and Fridays: skating, rap sessions, newsletter work sessions, theater parties, dancing, dinners, parties. The club encourages attendance at the monthly "Singular Event" dance, sponsored by Parents Without Partners; "enjoy the company of over 200 other singles" that Friday night. (See chapter 5.)

Dinners or potlucks are Saturday features. Weekends, Singles Together goes skiing, bicycling, rafting, camping, or hiking. Skiing and swimming trips are either close to home or far away. Experienced members lead all these jaunts.

❧

Circle Elite, PO Box 12552, Portland 97212 (Charles Goodwin, 230-1100) is a coed, dues-paying singles club run by Mr. Goodwin. A thousand are on his mailing list. Meant for professional people, it has an application form asking about occupation, education, and reputation. Someone belonging must then recommend you for membership. You may first attend events as a guest three times. Members are from 30 to 60 years old. Higher annual dues entitle you to certain Aero Club facilities.

Circle Elite holds Wednesday no-host cocktail parties and Thursday athletic nights (with light meals) at the **Aero Club of Oregon**, 804 SW Taylor, Portland (227-7400). The club has at least one monthly dinner dance, a variety of house and special parties, ski trips, and overseas tours.

❧

Altogether, these three big clubs afford you many opportunities for involvement and fun socializing. They and clubs discussed below provide many occasions for individuals to see one another as potential friends, not potential romantic attachments or potential competitors. "Singles helping other singles with emotional support, friendships, and knowing that there is someone who shares the good and bad times is what Servetus is all about," its newsletter declares.

Both Servetus and Singles Together, by the way, have active holiday schedules. They bring singles together for Thanksgiving dinners, New Year's Eve parties and drop-ins, Christmas dinners, all-day Christmas open houses, July 4 picnics, and other holiday times. Children are usually part of these gatherings. People share the preparations, the costs . . . and themselves.

SPECIAL INTEREST GROUPS

"Singles activities *per se* are not enough for me. There is just not enough common ground," says a 34-year-old woman. Yet in many groups (in this and the next section) participants share distinctive concerns, characteristics, or values. Here is the common ground she misses.

Parents Without Partners, PO Box 16204, Portland 97216 (774-7998); PO Box 949, Gresham 97030 (661-5998 or 666-4860); PO Box 782, Oregon City 97045 (232-8818); PO Box 1025, Beaverton 97075 (246-1925); and PO Box 2245,

Vancouver 98668 (1-206-254-3668 or 1-206-256-0191).

PWP has five local chapters expressly designed for single parents, custodial or not, of living children. There are groups for members' teenagers, too. After using a free, time-limited Courtesy Card, single parents must join PWP to participate. Any single, however, may attend its monthly dance, which draws over 200 dancers. (See chapter 5.)

PWP balances adult, family, and educational activities. Members share experiences, make new friends, and lend mutual aid while taking part in a common activity. One member writes that "the personal growth experienced by our active members ... is the best measurement" of Portland PWP success.

The 278-member Portland chapter, largest of the five, has one or more events *daily*. "Adult" events include "happy hours," card parties, volleyball, house parties, restaurant visits, and dancing. "Amigo" potlucks and small group discussions are for new members and Courtesy Card holders. They feature "friendship, a listening ear, a lot of encouragement to feel at home and to get involved." Coffee-discussions and other educational events are frequent. "Family" gatherings include volleyball, hot dog and movie nights, birthday parties, holiday celebrations, bowling, hikes, roller skating, pizza feeds, and boat trips. There are orientation, membership, and other meetings, too.

Portland PWP members range from their mid-twenties to their fifties; most are in their thirties and forties.

SOLO Center, 4225 NE Tillamook, Portland (287-0642) is a fee-based nonprofit resource center, not a singles club. It has its own house. The center wants "to help make single life more fulfilling, and the transition from married to single life successful." It conducts specialized programs for anyone who is undergoing or has undergone divorce or separation. To enrich the lives of all singles, it has Monday through Saturday evening drop-in and focused rap groups, classes, counseling, and social events at its house or elsewhere. Social workers and paraprofessionals lead many groups.

A free introductory session happens Monday evenings.

Wednesdays include events run by a lively "over 40" group. Another group buzzes through the local jazz scene on Saturday nights. The center is busy Friday nights. A get-acquainted time is followed by a presentation, then by dancing lessons. Dancing at clubs caps off the evening.

Subscribers get the monthly newspaper. For SOLO's House Sharing Service, see the last chapter.

Portland Skyliners, PO Box 713, Portland 97207, is a social club for tall adults over 21 years old. Women must be at least 5'10"; men, 6'2". Through activities such as house parties, dances, picnics, happy hours, dinners, beach parties, camping, and events with other Tall Clubs, it provides members with like interests ways to meet and develop friendships. It also furthers their concern as tall people. Almost all the 65 members are single. Ages range from 22 to 50, with most between 25 and 35.

Dynamic Singles, 3520 SE Yamhill, Portland (771-8478 or 233-4286) plans to reorganize. It has a weekly volleyball game.

RELIGIOUS-BASED GROUPS

By far, the greatest number of singles clubs in the area are the ones connected to religious groups. Many are small, with fewer than ten belonging. Some club activities turn out large numbers. A few of these groups have joint activities with organizations discussed in the previous section—Servetus for Single Adults, Singles Together, or SOLO Center.

Most clubs find their home and sense of being in religious institutions or pursuits, and club programs often relate to particular spiritual or religious concerns. Their low- and no-cost functions happen in and outside religious settings. If a group describes itself in terms of "fellowship," you can expect a blend of spiritual and social activities.

A church or synagogue may have a singles club not listed below. Several Vancouver churches reputed to sponsor them did not reply to my inquiries. Nonetheless, expect all these clubs to be eager for visitors and members. All of the following are open to *anyone* single, unless otherwise specified.

AFMS (Association of Formerly Married and Single), St.

Joseph's Catholic Church, 6600 Highland Dr., Vancouver (1-206-696-4407 or Jules, 1-206-254-9121) is an ecumenical club that provides an umbrella structure for both a divorce support group and a young adult singles group. They work "to support and enlarge their social, spiritual and emotional horizons." Its active calendar includes speakers, parties, theater and music nights, dining, dancing, beach and resort trips, cards, potlucks, game nights, and religious worship. Members are of all ages, and from 20 to 40 participate.

Association of Formerly Married Catholics are in Ascension Parish Center, 7507 SE Yamhill, Portland (256-3897); St. Patrick Church, 1623 NW 19th, Portland (286-3929); St. Cecilia Church, 5105 SW Franklin, Beaverton (644-2619); Holy Trinity Church, 13715 SW Walker Rd., Beaverton (643-9528); and for the Southwest Vicarate, contact Bob, 961 Lake Front Rd., Lake Oswego (636-2240). The Association emphasizes spiritual, moral, and emotional support for the divorced, separated, widowed, and other interested single persons. Chapters usually meet weekly for speakers, films, and social events such as parties and picnics. Gatherings may include children. Pastoral counseling is available. Group size varies from ten to 36; members are older than 35.

Canby Christian Singles, 10978 S. Mulino Rd., Canby (Doris, 266-6609) provides Christian fellowship to its 15 to 20 members. It meets monthly for a Saturday breakfast in a Canby restaurant and monthly for a Saturday evening potluck. Ages range from 35 to 75, with most between 50 and 75.

Christian Single Adults, 2180 NW 14th, Gresham (666-5862) arranges weekly social events emphasizing Christian spirituality and fellowship. It has speakers, singing groups, picnics, and other activities. Its 50 participants range from 40 to 60 years old, with most in their fifties.

ESP (Episcopal Singles of Portland), c/o Cathedral of St. John. 6300 SW Nicol Rd., Portland (Pat, 245-3777) sponsors functions throughout Episcopal Church parishes in the area. ESP advances personal spiritual and non-spiritual needs and growth. While primarily for singles, anyone, regardless of religion or marital status, may join. It has monthly potlucks, speakers, discussions, games, hikes, beach retreats, picnics, concert nights, tours, and other events. Some include children. About 500 belong between the ages of 25 and 70. As many as 50 participate in an activity. Most are either between 25 and 35 or 50 and 60 years old.

FOCAS (Fellowship of Christian Adult Singles), 1315 SE 20th, Portland (Joan, 231-5020) is an Assembly of God-sponsored group for singles wanting fellowship in a Christian environment. Sunday afternoon speakers and inspirational music draw more than 100. Thursday evening groups for personal growth and spiritual development attract between 15 and 20. Twice-monthly Wednesday lunch-time fellowship programs in downtown Portland are devoted to speakers, music, or growth sharing. Members range from 25 to 65, with most older than 30.

Genesis Single Adult Fellowship, 2030 SW 185th, Aloha (Art or Sharon, 642-2054) provides an interdenominational Christian-based fellowship to meet personal spiritual and social needs and serve as a support group for single adults. Platonic but intimate relationships are encouraged; drugs and alcohol, barred. Genesis provides speakers, rap sessions, hikes, picnics, potlucks, campouts, skiing, bowling, swimming, sing-alongs, and other events. As many as 50 participate, from age 25 to 50; most are in their thirties and forties.

Hinneni, Laurel Park Bible Chapel, 621 NE 76th, Portland (Bruce McNicol, 254-5297) is for singles interested in spiritual renewal, social activities, and community service projects. Regular meetings on Sunday evenings feature Bible study, prayer, and singing. Seasonally, there are retreats, community projects, and a variety of social events. There are about 90 members between 20 and 40 years old; events usually draw 50 to 60.

Hinson Singles Network, Hinson Baptist Church, 1137 SE 20th, Portland (Rev. Lauterbach, 232-1156) provides opportunities for developing personal relationships among singles and ways for them to mature as Christians. Thirteen Bible Study classes, attracting 185, meet away from the church. The Network offers a number of social activities weekly. Some 400 belong, from 18 to 40 years old.

MJCC Singles Group, Mittleman Jewish Community Center, 6651 SW Capitol Hwy., Portland (244-0111) has speakers, discussions, picnics, potlucks, brunches, game and theater nights, camping, downhill and cross-country skiing, rafting, Sabbath dinners, and other events. The 125 members range from their twenties into their forties.

Mixed Company, First United Methodist Church, 1838 SW Jefferson, Portland (228-3195 or Max, 645-5829 or Iola, 288-3571) has church potlucks on the third Saturday evening each month as well as occasional social events. It encourages friendships among participants. Its 15 to 20 members range upwards from 34 years of age; most are in their fifties.

New Hope Positive Singles, New Hope Community Church, 11731 SE Stevens Rd., Milwaukie (659-5683 or from Portland 774-8851) combines Christian spiritual pursuits with social, educational, and relational activities. A total of 300 to 400 will participate in its many events during any week. Most are between 35 and 45 years old.

New Life-Soul Support, St. Henry Catholic Church, 346 NW First, Gresham (Sister Phyllis, 666-3791) is a Tuesday evening support group for Catholics and non-Catholics experiencing widowhood, divorce, or separation. It helps reintegrate them into parish life. The group has occasional social events. The seven to 15 members are mostly between 25 and 50 years old.

Our Savior's Singles, Our Savior's Lutheran Church, 1040 C Ave., Lake Oswego (635-4563) ministers in a Christian context to single adults. It has Sunday morning lesson-discussions, monthly rap sessions, Sunday brunches (children included), adult weekend retreats, and other growth and social activities. From 15 to 40 participate, ranging in age from 30 to 60; most are between 35 and 45.

Portland Chancellor Club, PO Box 162, Portland 97207, is for single Roman Catholics between 21 and 40; non-Catholics are associate members. The club pursues social, spiritual, intellectual, and recreational goals. It has monthly meetings and smaller groups. Each third Saturday night of the month, it has a public dance at the Knights of Columbus Hall, 532 SE

Ankeny in Portland. Seventy to 80 belong, and 60 to 70 come as guests. Most members are between 25 and 35 years old.

Roaring Twenties (And Then Some), First United Methodist Church, 1838 SW Jefferson, Portland (228-3195) is for singles 18 to 35 years old who attend this church, as well as young adult visitors. In addition to monthly Sunday restaurant brunch planning meetings, the club sponsors various social and recreational activities and church and community projects: hikes, theater and movie parties, for instance, and events shared with Young Adult Ministry (see below). Upwards of 20 belong, mainly between 25 and 30 years old.

Single Focus, Milwaukie First Baptist Church, 10750 SE 42nd, Milwaukie (654-9593 or Phil, 659-1081 or Hazel, 653-0082) gathers singles interested in Christian fellowship for religious study and spiritual growth, trips, and various social events. It has picnics, movie nights, bowling, camping, beach parties, retreats, and smaller get-togethers. Its 20 to 25 participants range from 21 to 36, with most between 24 and 30 years old.

Singles, Beaverton Foursquare Church, 13565 SW Walker Rd., Beaverton (644-9104) has 150 to 350 participants. Its spiritual emphasis includes Friday evening Bible study (drawing 150), weekend retreats, and missionary outreach to several nations. Fostering its goal of "to grow in relationships with others," Singles has Wednesday morning breakfasts, after-service coffee times, ski trips, parties, beach trips, and a summer visit to the San Juan Islands. Members range from 20 to 55, with most between 25 and 35 years old.

Sojourners, St. Luke Lutheran Church, 6835 SW 46th, Portland (246-2325) offers fellowship to Christian singles and young marrieds. It has weekly Bible study on Tuesdays, monthly community service projects, and such social events as potlucks, picnics, skiing, and camping. About 20 belong, ranging from 22 to 35 years old.

Upwards Trails, Troutdale. (See chapter 3.)

U.S. With PEACE, East Hill Church of the Foursquare Gospel, 701 N. Main, Gresham (Gary or Phil, 661-4444) is a support group for single parents and those experiencing divorce, separation, or other traumas. Open to church attendees, it sponsors such events as beach retreats, snow days, and camping. Some activities include children. From 15 to 30 participate, ranging in age from 30 to 45 years old, with most in their late thirties.

Valley Singles, c/o Valley Community United Presbyterian Church, 8060 SW Brentwood, Portland (292-3537) provides Christian fellowship and spiritual growth through church and social activities. The first Friday each month, members have a meeting-potluck and perhaps hear a speaker. Sundays, they eat brunch in a Beaverton restaurant with Servetus for Single Adults members. That evening, they go dancing and dining together. Valley Singles also has rap sessions, card and table games, theater and musical evenings, parties, golfing, picnics, a beach weekend, dining out parties, and other events. More than 85 belong. Events draw from 12 to 24 individuals. Members range between 45 and 65 years old, with most in their fifties.

West Portland Solo's, West Portland United Methodist Church, 4729 SW Taylors Ferry Rd., Portland (Rick, 636-7053) is interested in the meaning of the Christian Gospel for everyday life. It has a Sunday School discussion class, social occasions, and retreats. Its eight to ten members range in age from 40 to 55.

Young Adult Group, St. Henry Catholic Church, 346 NW First, Gresham (666-3791) focuses on Christian development and fellowship, mutual aid, and social activities. It meets second and fourth Sundays of the month and holds a monthly coffee house. Its five to ten members are in their twenties.

Young Adult Ministry, c/o First Presbyterian Church, 1200 SW Alder, Portland, stresses social and spiritual opportunities of an ecumenical Christian nature. YAM supplements young adult groups in area churches (which distribute its monthly newsletter) and seeks the unchurched. It has Bible study, weekly volleyball, fellowship and game nights, swimming, potlucks, hikes, picnics, dances, and other weekly events. It conducts four annual retreats. About 30 people (mostly single) are active in it. They are from 18 to 40 plus; most are in their twenties.

The Young Singles, Village Baptist Church, 330 SW Murray Blvd., Beaverton (Bob, 643-6511) helps meet the social and spiritual needs of young singles, including equipping them to help others. After Sunday services, 45 members meet elsewhere for Bible study and fellowship. Weekly, this group, mainly composed of those from 23 to 35 years old, gathers for such social and recreational events as coed volleyball, men's basketball, potlucks, speakers, and parties. Over 70 go on its annual rafting trip.

DECEMBER, 1982

LAST MONTH

S	M	T	W	T	F	S
			1	2	3	4
5	6	7	8	9	10	11
12	13	14	15	16	17	18
19	20	21	22	23	24	25
26	27	28	29	30	31	

NEXT MONTH

November 1982
S	M	T	W	T	F	S
	1	2	3	4	5	6
7	8	9	10	11	12	13
14	15	16	17	18	19	20
21	22	23	24	25	26	27
28	29	30				

January 1983
S	M	T	W	T	F	S
						1
2	3	4	5	6	7	8
9	10	11	12	13	14	15
16	17	18	19	20	21	22
23	24	25	26	27	28	29
30	31					

SUNDAY
346/019
12
Comedy open mike
at tavern 9 pm

MONDAY
347/018
13

TUESDAY
348/017
14
Call about weekend
at coast

WEDNESDAY
349/016
15
● NEW MOON
Ballroom Dancing
8 pm

THURSDAY
350/015
16

FRIDAY
351/014
17

SATURDAY
352/013
18
Live jazz - second show

DEC. 12 TO 18, 1982

5

BARS, CLUBS, AND DANCING

BARS AND CLUBS

One of the few institutions expressly designed for singles to meet flourishes in the Portland area: the singles bar. It serves liquor or just wine or beer and, always, non-alcoholic beverages. Clubs have live or recorded music for listening or dancing. At some bars, patrons are the entertainment.

Bars and clubs want the singles trade. A number solicit it with free *hors d'oeuvres* or lower-priced drinks after work. People come from the neighborhood, nearby workplaces, or farther away. Patrons may or may not be of like age or style. Do you want a crowd mainly between 21 and 27 years old? Rock music clubs are the place. Do you want live jazz on a regular basis? Some 20 clubs feature it, mostly soft jazz and danceable fusion.

Singles bars and clubs may be great for you, contrary to some negative opinions. "Since I have started going to bars," a 21-year-old woman says, "I have really met lots of new people;" some she dated. A 33-year-old woman relates, "I stopped looking for a man years ago. Now I have fun," especially by going to clubs for dancing.

In a national survey of American singles, *Singles*, one out of four men and almost one out of five women reported that they first met most of the people they dated in bars and clubs. "I think that there are a higher quantity of single people who have met people in Portland bars and date them than they are ready to admit," speculates a 28-year-old woman who savors local clubs.

Who really enjoys singles bars? Simenauer and Carroll's national survey of 3,000 mainly white middle-class Americans, *Singles*, outlined two profiles. In the first group (much the largest), the average satisfied bargoers are high school educated, younger than 35, divorced or, among women, also never married. They work in blue-collar jobs and earn middle- or lower-middle level incomes.

A distinct minority of singles bargoers form a different profile, according to this study. They are better educated and more affluent, and certain bars and clubs cater to them.

These findings about crowds seem generally valid for the clubs and bars described by Haughen and Busch in *Portland After Dark: Book Two*. They identified and evaluated 150 Portland-area gathering spots, noting those which were popular among singles and those which were "body exchanges." Consult their or similar books listed in the back of *Single in Portland*.

Singles' hangouts have come and gone since Haughen and Busch's 1980 book. For instance, Luis' LaBamba opened—then closed. Sack's, Earth, Foghorn, Accuardi's, Delevan's, and Casey's Corral closed. **The Main Place**, 101 SW Main, Portland (228-4224) and **Father's American Broiler and Nightclub**, 309 SW Third, Portland (227-5492) opened for an affluent crowd. **Cassidy's**, 1331 SW Washington, Portland (223-0054) began drawing singles interested in the arts, writing, and journalism, "the disciplined counterculture crowd," says a 37-year-old male admirer.

Note that bars and clubs rank number one in controversy among American singles. Many here shun them. Some singles try them briefly and leave unsatisfied. Critics associate them with an exaggerated sexuality and the absence of compensating virtues. These images prevent many from ever testing the reality—and therefore recognizing any good points. Or, if they do give it a try, they are apt to misinterpret what they see.

Much depends on your expectations. Singles bars and clubs have a definite advantage: everyone arrives there specifically to meet and be with others. Don't feel guilty that you share that goal—that kind of thinking won't help.

Either men or women may take the initiative. Either may start a conversation without being deemed forward. Either may walk up to another. *Or away from the other.* For neither the person nor the place should make you feel like somebody you are not. Individuals need not tolerate being grabbed. (Remember, though, that in this setting body contact is not necessarily the same as being hassled.) Employees, if asked or signalled, will help extricate someone from a sticky situation.

Whether you go alone or with a friend is up to you, but you owe it to yourself to arrive relaxed and ready for enjoyment. Trusted companions may help override any early tensions or later hassles. A 29-year-old man likes to have friends around initially for moral support; soon, he is happily on his own meeting women. A 25-year-old man goes with a platonic woman friend; they decide beforehand whether or not they will leave together. A 28-year-old woman volunteers another perspective: "If you want to meet a guy, and you go with another woman to a bar, the chances are 50-50. But if you are alone, its 100%."

Try neighborhood bars, several single women advise. Many are definitely coed. One woman calls her favorite neighborhood hangout a little community of friendly customers, even if the bar looks sleazy. Neighborhood bars may have their own sports teams worth joining.

Again, what are your expectations? Are you there for a sexual partner, or the beginning of a deep, loving relationship, or just a good time in the bar? If you seek that special person now—this very afternoon or evening—your chances are every bit as good—or as poor—in a bar as in any other setting.

Watch out for preconceptions. If you come thinking that only losers go to bars, you lower your own self-esteem and unfairly prejudge potential companions, and you certainly won't enjoy yourself.

Once you are there, give the place a chance. Some people may be rushing around trying to meet the maximum number of people in the minimum amount of time. You'll find a thick skin helpful at first. If someone is looking past your shoulder, or mumbling replies to you, it could be because he or she is shy or nervous. Some people will try to impress you with their accomplishments, intelligence, or status; bring kindness for dumb remarks. And after you have been there a while, if the place is not comfortable for you, *leave*. You're in control here.

You are also in control of how significantly you wish to get involved with anyone you may meet there. Good sense and basic cautions are called for. Forty percent of the single women in Simenauer and Carroll's national study report having suffered some kind of mental or physical abuse in singles bars or during what transpired afterward.

A 21-year-old Portland woman suggests not baring secrets immediately and not exchanging last names or phone numbers. Get those of the men, she adds. Share at the same level of intimacy. If you connect, think about leaving together (in separate cars) for another public place, such as a coffee shop or restaurant. Or arrange a future meeting in a public place. In a singles bar as anywhere else, a man or woman determines his or her involvement and risk.

So if you are ready for the clubs, check local newspaper entertainment sections for who is performing. For greater detail, see *Two Louies*, *Prevue*, or *Positively Entertainment*, free publications. As dramatic changes occur in programs—and clubs open and close—it is best to call ahead.

DANCING

Ballroom, pattern, New Wave, rock, country honky-tonk, folk, square—whatever your favorite dancing, you don't need a partner. Every evening, and several afternoons, you can go dancing somewhere in the metropolitan area.

Where? Many singles organizations go dancing as a group or have dances you may attend. (See chapter 4.) So do many of the clubs and associations described in chapter 3. Or go dancing at the night clubs, discussed in the previous section. "I will pick out a man I saw dancing with a couple of women already, so I know he can dance and wants to dance" rather than show off his clothes or just sit and look. "That way," says a 33-year-old woman who loves to dance, "I hope to pick someone who doesn't expect anything other than dancing."

Dancers come for the fun and company. They arrive alone,

with friends, or as pairs (but not necessarily planning to leave together). Normally, anyone may ask another to dance. "Some dances done" at folk dances "are mixers, where partners change a lot," says a 29-year-old man. "People at these dances are incredibly friendly" and "lots of single people attend."

All it takes is asking and volunteering your name. "Where else can you see, feel, smell, and be active with someone you just met? You can tell alot about someone" dancing, and "you can dance off any nervousness you might feel at the same time," says this man. Dancing also has time limits. Dance a lot, or sit out dances talking to your new partner. And, always, expect to meet many new people, if you don't let bashfulness get in your way.

Many organizations and groups, as well as commercial studios, teach dancing, "and people help you learn more" as you dance, says a 61-year-old woman. Dances charge nothing, modestly, or slightly higher fees.

Events calendars in the press and newsletters tell you of many dances. For additional information on clubs with dancing, consult the free *Two Louies*, *Prevue*, or *Positively Entertainment*. For updates on square dance locations and times call the **Portland Area Council of Square Dancers** at 761-1709 or **Tualatin Valley Council Square Dance Association** at 244-8341. But remember to *call ahead* for everything listed here as days, times, and locations change rapidly.

Ballroom, Pattern, Disco, and Old Time Dancing
(may go alone):

TUESDAYS
"Goodtime Singles Casual Dance" at Portland Eagles Club, 8835 SW 30th, Portland (246-4255).

WEDNESDAYS
Servetus for Single Adults singles-only dances at clubhouse, 2005 SE 82nd, Rm. 6, Portland (774-7337).

Old Time dancing at Eagles Bldg., 8401 N. Ivanhoe, Portland (286-8787).

Dancing at Vancouver Eagles Club, 8803 NE 76th, Vancouver (1-206-892-2158). Call about nonmember entrance requirements.

Ballroom and swing dancing, Ockley Green Community School, 6031 N. Montana, Portland (285-8269).

(First and Third) Dancing at North Clackamas Park, Oregon 224 and Rusk Rd., Clackamas.

THURSDAYS

Servetus for Single Adults reserves a singles table at The Woodshed, 16015 SE Stark, Portland, for dancing most Thursdays. Information: 774-7337.

FRIDAYS

Dancing at Melody Lane Ballroom, 615 SE Alder, Portland (232-2759).

(Second and Fourth) Servetus for Single Adults singles-only dancing at different hotels, clubs, and ballrooms. Information: 774-7337.

Dancing at University Park Community Center, 9009 N. Foss, Portland (289-2414).

(Once monthly) Parents Without Partners singles-only dancing at Portland Eagles Club, 8835 SW 30th, Portland (246-4255). Information: 654-1783.

(First and Third) Sesame Club's Big Band dancing at Norse Hall, 111 NE 11th, Portland (236-3401).

(Second and Fourth) Old Time dancing at Hillsboro Grange Hall, 245 SE Third, Hillsboro.

SATURDAYS

Dancing to Big Band music at Melody Lane Ballroom, 615 SE Alder, Portland (232-2759).

Old Time dancing at Washington Grange, Pumpkin Ridge, four miles north of North Plains.

Dancing at Sellwood Masonic Bldg., 7126 SE Milwaukie, Portland (232-9925).

Dancing at Eagles Lodge, 4904 SE Hawthorne, Portland (232-7505).

(Second and Fourth) Dancing at North Clackamas Park,

Oregon 224 and Rusk Rd., Clackamas.

(First and Third) Dancing at Norse Hall, 111 NE 11th, Portland (236-3401).

(Third) Dancing at Knights of Columbus Hall, 532 SE Ankeny, Portland (236-9388).

For the over-40 ballroom dancer, **Sesame Dance Club**, c/o Norse Hall, 111 NE 11th, Portland has dances to Big Band sounds and assorted social events. Its twice-monthly Saturday public dances at Norse Hall (see above) are but part of its schedule. The club joins other dance clubs for events. Up to 100 participate. Most members are in their fifties, and 50 to 60% are single.

Square Dancing (may go alone):

WEDNESDAYS
Bachelor-Bachelorette Square Dance Club at the Square Dancing Center, 3131 SE 50th, Portland (774-3066).

THURSDAYS
(Second and Fourth) Circul-8-N-Singles at Leddy Grange, NW Cornell Rd. at Saltzman Rd., Cedar Mill.

FRIDAYS
(First and Third) Spares and Pairs at Sunnyside Grange, SE 132nd and Sunnyside Rd., Clackamas (Don, 761-2493).

(First and Third) The Singles Square at 5930 N. Interstate Ave., Portland.

(Second) Square Dancing at Oaks Park Ballroom, foot of SE Spokane, Portland (246-0264).

(Second and Fourth) Fun Lovers at Oak Grove Community Hall, Oak Grove.

(Fourth) Square and Contra Dancing at Multnomah Art Center, 7688 SW Capitol Hwy., Portland (Rick, 777-3630). Dances are taught. Children are welcome.

SUNDAYS
(Third and Fourth) Swinging Squares at Aloha Grange, 185th and TV Hwy., Aloha.

Folk Dancing (may go alone):

MONDAYS

Balkan Folk Dancing at Fremont United Methodist Church, 2620 NE Fremont, Portland (222-1322). Lessons precede dancing.

(October to June) English Country Dancing at 212 Shattuck Hall, Portland State University, SW Broadway and Hall, Portland (Dick, 282-6004). Dances are taught.

TUESDAYS

Clog Dancing at Marquam Community Hall, 107th and SW Capitol Hwy., Portland (625-2258). Some basic experience is preferred.

Irish Dancing, St. Rita's Parish Hall, 10029 NE Prescott, Portland (227-5895). Beginners are welcome.

International Folk Dancing at Reed College Sports Center, 3203 SE Woodstock Blvd., Portland (771-1112). Lessons precede dancing.

Medieval and Renaissance Dancing at Marshall Center, 1009 E. McLoughlin Blvd., Vancouver (1-206-696-8236). Dances are taught. Women are asked to wear long dresses.

WEDNESDAYS

Clog Dancing at First Christian Church, 1812 Main, Vancouver (1-206-693-2519). Basic experience is helpful.

Scottish Country Dancing at Marshall Center, 1009 E. McLoughlin Blvd., Vancouver. Information: Marge, 1521 NE 97th, Vancouver. Class precedes dancing. Low- or no-heel shoes are advised.

THURSDAYS

Israeli Folk Dancing at Mittleman Jewish Community Center, 6651 SW Capitol Hwy., Portland (224-0111).

International Folk Dancing at 7045 SW Taylors Ferry Rd., Portland (246-1152 or Pat, 288-0840).

FRIDAYS

International Folk Dancing at 212 Shattuck Hall, Portland

State University, SW Broadway and Hall, Portland (229-4433). Lessons precede dancing.

(First) Contra Dancing at Multnomah Art Center, 7688 SW Capitol Hwy., Portland (248-3333). Information: 641-0250 or 282-6004. Dances are taught. Children are welcome.

(Third, from September to June) Irish Dancing at Portland Police Athletic Association Hall, 618 SE Alder, Portland (253-0206 or 227-5895). Lessons precede dancing.

SATURDAYS

Clog Dancing at Multnomah Art Center, 7688 SW Capitol Hwy., Portland (248-3333 or Alison, 282-8816).

(First, from October to June) Scottish Country Dancing at Lincoln Savings and Loan, 12320 SW First, Beaverton (Ian or Florrie, 644-5508). Older children are welcome. Bring snacks.

(First) Irish and American Dancing, contact Dan or Joan, 308 NE Repass, Vancouver (1-206-694-3545).

(First and third) Scandinavian Dancing (mainly) at Norse Hall, 111 NE 11th, Portland (654-6629). Lessons precede dancing.

(Second) Contra Dancing at Westminster Presbyterian Church, 1624 NE Hancock, Portland (641-0205 or 282-6004). Dances are taught. Children are welcome.

(Second, from September to June) Scottish Country Dancing at St. Johns YWCA, 8010 N. Charleston, Portland (Don, 252-3570 or Kathy, 288-9436). Some teaching is done. Children are welcome.

SUNDAYS

International Folk Dancing at Fulton Park Community Center, 68 SW Miles, Portland (233-2307). Children and beginners are welcome.

(First and third) Greek Dancing at Trinity Greek Orthodox Church, 3131 NE Glisan, Portland (234-0468). Lessons precede dancing.

(Twice Monthly) Gay and Lesbian Folk Dancing at 212 Shattuck Hall, Portland State University, SW Broadway and Hall, Portland (226-0490). Beginners are welcome.

FEBRUARY, 1983

S	M	T	W	T	F	S
		1	2	3	4	5
6	7	8	9	10	11	12
13	14	15	16	17	18	19
20	21	22	23	24	25	26
27	28					

LAST MONTH

January 1983
S M T W T F S
                    1
2 3 4 5 6 7 8
9 10 11 12 13 14 15
16 17 18 19 20 21 22
23 24 25 26 27 28 29
30 31

NEXT MONTH

March 1983
S M T W T F S
      1 2 3 4 5
6 7 8 9 10 11 12
13 14 15 16 17 18 19
20 21 22 23 24 25 26
27 28 29 30 31

SUNDAY
044/321
● **13**
NEW MOON

MONDAY
045/320
14

Valentine's Day

Craft Class 6:30 pm

TUESDAY
046/319
15

Sample Intro Fitness
class — join?

WEDNESDAY
047/318
16

Ash Wednesday

Brown Bag concert
at Old Church

THURSDAY
048/317
17

FRIDAY
049/316
18

SATURDAY
050/315
19

Saturday Market

FEB. 13 TO 19, 1983

6

MORE DELIGHTS

OUTDOOR PLACES AND EVENTS

Wonderful parks, trails, and tracks. Magnificent rivers, hills, mountains, and forests. Organized and spontaneous events in splendid settings. All lure hordes of singles to outdoor places throughout our metropolitan region.

The city of Portland alone has 160 parks, mostly neighborhood ones, offering 80 miles of running and hiking trails, three jogging tracks, and four exercise courses. In Vancouver, **Fort Vancouver Park** provides a "good meeting place while lounging about in the summer," according to a 30-year-old woman. Portland singles echo that feeling about many of their parks, including **Laurelhurst Park**. Individuals comfortably stroll alone in such popular places as the **Portland Rose Test Garden** and **Japanese Garden**, adjacent in **Washington Park**, or in the less-known, but larger, **Peninsula Park Rose Garden**.

Mild weather brings outdoor lunchers to downtown Portland spots. They gravitate to the **South Park Blocks**, **Lovejoy Fountain**, **Ira Keller Fountain**, **Pettygrove Park**, **O'Bryant Square**, and the **Plaza Blocks**. PSU students and staff mix freely with downtowners on **Portland State University**'s campus. If you stick with one comfortable spot, you soon recognize fellow lunchers from nearby and start to chat.

Single lovers of the arts seem to flourish in the summertime. Portland's **Washington Park** hosts an extensive **Summer Festival** of free drama, dancing, and concerts from mid-July through August. Arrive early for the better-known performers.

Free concerts grace early summer evenings in Portland at

Mount Tabor Park, **Laurelhurst Park**, and in the **South Park Blocks**. Noontime downtown concerts take place in **O'Bryant Square** and **Chapman Square** in Portland and in downtown Vancouver parks.

Beaverton, Vancouver, and Gresham city parks also sponsor popular summer musical series. **Tryon Creek State Park**, 11321 SW Terwilliger Blvd., Portland (636-4550) has Sunday afternoon summer concerts.

Outdoor concerts are "super places for meeting people," many singles report. Skillful placement of blanket or lawnchair is one key. One woman attends Washington Park concerts and "Your Zoo, And All That Jazz" concerts with a few female friends. They put down their blanket strategically near a group of attractive, and hopefully single, men. Sharing extra cups and drinks breaks the ice for friendly talk.

Nature or fitness lovers may be less absorbed in their activities than they appear. "You can meet people when you're running," a serious woman jogger reports. Joggers smile, race ahead, and wait for the other person to catch up and then chat as they take a break together. "People run in groups all the time," she says. They are also eager to share party information and invitations.

Singles use the two-mile exercise and jogging track in **Duniway Park**. Other favorite trails are in **Washington** and **Forest Parks** and, on the eastside, near **Reed College** and at **Oaks Bottom**, **Sellwood Park**, and **Mount Tabor Park**. Singles jam the jogging track at **Glendoveer Golf Course**, 14015 NE Glisan, Portland, according to a 28-year-old woman jogger.

Singles pedal as well as pound the pavement. Bicyclers attend rides sponsored by local parks and recreation departments and many clubs and institutions listed in this book. During summers, bicycle and motorcycle riders gather at **Mount Tabor Park**.

Hiking can be a solitary or collective venture. Group hikes are convivial and often educational. Some **Portland Parks and Recreation Bureau** hikes need preregistration; call 248-4018. And check through chapters 3, 4, and 6 for additional groups which sponsor hikes.

"Day Trippers" leave for various places from **Tryon Creek State Park**, 11321 SW Terwilliger Blvd., Portland (636-4550) during fall and spring. **Leach Botanical Park**, 6704 SE 122nd, Portland (761-9503 or 760-6618) has free guided walks. **Hoyt Arboretum** has free guided walks leaving all seasons from its Visitor Center, 4000 SW Fairview, Portland (228-8732). Brisk summer walks through downtown Portland start weekday evenings in front of the **Multnomah County Library**, 801 SW Tenth, Portland (Kathleen, 231-8899); there is a small fee.

Walking your dog is a classic way to meet similar-minded people. Old-fashioned advice books suggested faking dog leash entanglement, but that's tacky.

Or go fly a kite. It acts as a magnet for adults, not just children. One man reports meeting his future wife as he flew a kite in a park. Artists with pads or easels in the outdoors or museums likewise attract commentators.

Interested in possible beach companions? A 21-year-old woman advises trying the beaches at **Kelley Point Park**, where the Columbia and Willamette rivers meet, and on the Sandy River. Singles in their twenties dominate the beach at Sauvie Island, according to a 28-year-old man.

Snow-worshipers as well as sun-worshipers will find new friends at **Timberline**, **Mount Hood Meadows**, **Multorpor**, and other nearby ski resorts. **Timberline** (from Portland, call 226-7979) has a Friday package deal for singles which includes bus transportation there and back, lift tickets, rentals, and ski lessons. A dance ends the evening.

Saturday Market, **Artquake**, and **KGW-Neighborfair** are great places for frolic. Singles by the score report friendly mingling and meeting there. Weekends from April to Christmas, **Saturday Market** spreads its wares out next to **Waterfront Park** near Portland's Burnside Bridge. A 28-year-old rollerskater routes herself through it. "Invariably you will meet other rollerskaters, or people will begin conversations with you because you have on rollerskates rather than shoes."

Artquake draws crowds into downtown Portland one September weekend and to related programs afterward. **KGW-**

Neighborfair brings over 300,000 to **Waterfront Park** on a July Sunday. It is, says a 25-year-old man, "a great place to meet people" when wandering between booths and events. Its "Folkfest" section offers a tasty variety of ethnic music, dance, crafts, and food.

Portland **Oktoberfest** finds folk cavorting in **Holladay Park** each September while **Autumnfest** enlivens the Old Town/Burnside neighborhood in late summer. Smaller fairs, festivals, and bazaars pop up throughout the metropolitan region in all seasons. **Park Block Revels**, for example, overflows to nearby museums, churches, theaters, restaurants, and Portland State University the first Sunday in December. Crowds enjoy free theater, music, dance, art, photography, film, and refreshments. They also have a chance to meet Northwest authors, who autograph their books at the Oregon Historical Society.

People at all these events clearly have lots of fun. They search out bargains, learn something new, and soak up food, drink, music, and the crowds. Like many before you, you may find these events excellent places for meeting people. But even if not, you are bound to enjoy yourself.

INDOOR PLACES AND EVENTS

Portland State University provides free "Brown Bag" noontime concerts once or twice weekly in 75 Lincoln Hall, SW Broadway at Market, in Portland. It also schedules free noontime speakers. For information, call 229-4074. Wednesdays at noon, **The Old Church**, 1422 SW 11th, Portland (222-2031) has free "Sack Lunch" concerts. **The Blanchard Education Service Center**, 501 N. Dixon, Portland (249-2000) has twice-monthly, free noontime concerts on Wednesdays. **Portland Art Museum**, 1219 SW Park, Portland (226-2811) presents "Art Sandwiched In" there or next door at the **Masonic Temple**. These are free noontime talks. People bring lunches to all these weekly events.

Think about dropping in at a nearby **YMCA** or **YWCA** (see next section) for a vigorous game of basketball or volleyball or a swim during your lunch period or after work. Some activities are coed, some not.

Singles with children readily meet other adults, with or without children, at many public places and events. This happens, for instance, at the **Oregon Historical Center**, 1230 SW Park, Portland (222-1741) and at three institutions clustered together off Portland's Canyon Rd.—**Oregon Museum of Science and Industry**, **Washington Park Zoo**, and **Western Forestry Center**. (See "classes".) A 29-year-old man who takes a young nephew to such places, to parks, and to **Oaks Park**, at the east end of the Sellwood Bridge, finds that he often meets female single parents. They are impressed when they find out that the boy is not his child, that he is single.

What about attending a church or synagogue? Social hours before or after welcome visitors. Local religious bodies are increasingly sensitive to single people, not just to families. Many have singles clubs (see chapter 4) or widowhood or other support groups (see chapter 8). No one need be "with" someone to attend any of their services or functions.

Similarly, you don't need a date to go to museums, galleries, lectures, movies, plays, or concerts. "Every woman ought to learn how to go to all places comfortably alone," declares a 34-year-old woman. If you are feeling shy, go one or two times with a companion. "Regulars" soon recognize and talk to one another. The many free programs—films, speakers, and concerts—at public libraries may be settings to practice going alone to something enjoyable.

Singles throng theaters, concert halls, and movie houses. Waiting lines and intermissions tend to be chatty. Join in if you see someone you know or begin a casual conversation, perhaps about the performance. In movie theater lobbies, singles linger at the **Fine Arts**, 2021 SE Hawthorne, Portland (232-7005); **Movie House**, 1220 SW Taylor, Portland (222-4595)—it has chairs, newspapers, and chess boards; **Clinton Street**, 2522 SE Clinton, Portland (238-8899); **Cinema 21**, 616 NW 21st, Portland (223-4722); **Fifth Avenue Cinema**, 510 SW Hall, Portland (224-6038); and at the **Portland Art Museum**, 1219 SW Park, Portland (226-2811) before or after Northwest Film

Study Center presentations. Serious movie content is the hall-mark of their presentations.

Art museums and art galleries are fabled meeting places during regular hours or special events. Exhibit openings "are social situations set up so people can talk as well as look at the art," a 28-year-old man observes. Those discussing the art are usually patrons; those around the food and drink, with friends in tow, usually the artists. And what a variety of art to choose from! Some 40 galleries and museums, plus numerous libraries, colleges, even restaurants and movie houses, exhibit art in the metropolitan area.

Most openings are public and publicized. Few galleries or museums require membership. However, by belonging to the **Portland Art Association**, 1219 SW Park, Portland (226-2811), you are a member both of the Portland Art Museum and the Northwest Film Society. So you may attend special receptions to preview museum exhibits and film festivals.

Membership in the **Portland Center for the Visual Arts**, 117 NW Fifth, Portland (222-7107) also entitles you to exhibition previews and other special events. PCVA features contemporary visual and performing arts, including theater, dance, new music, and jazz.

Membership in the **Northwest Artists' Workshop**, 522 NW 12th, Portland (220-0435) means enjoying an array by regional artists of new and experimental art, new music, jazz, rock and ethnic music, poetry readings, dance, and film and video presentations.

A longtime member of both PCVA and NWAW reports that the latter "is less well-heeled and more youngish, more of them in their twenties and thirties, than the PCVA crowd."

Membership in the **Oregon Symphony Association**, 813 SW Alder, Portland (241-8170) brings invitations to open rehearsals and a special contributors' concert.

Local lectures, workshops, and conferences offer you personal and professional development. They also have distinct social flavorings: social hours and name tags; animated talk in lobbies and at exhibits; people clustering around groups and companies promoting themselves.

A 41-year-old woman enjoys "going to events, like lectures." Figuring out which attractive men appear single, she sits beside her choice and begins a conversation. When these meetings occur on campuses or in libraries, she also checks their bulletin boards, student newspapers, and announcements to learn of future offerings.

Jazz, folk, country and western, and pop musical concerts attract large crowds of singles who get off on the music and one another. Try, for instance, the "Public Folk Music Concerts" on the first and third Thursday early evenings each month at the **Metropolitan Learning Center**, 2033 NW Glisan, Portland (241-0299). Children are welcome. At these casual gatherings, singles seem to move around the fringes or unobtrusively locate their seats or blankets near likely looking new companions.

Don't underestimate the social potential of everyday places, like cafes, stores, and laundromats. Restaurants with cozy seating encourage meeting new people, for example. Anyone may ask a stranger to share his or her table in such settings, remarks a 31-year-old woman. People lean across to talk to somebody at the next table. One way that she opens a conversation is to talk about any book, magazine, or newspaper either is reading.

A good breakfast (or lunch or dinner) place for this to happen, according to another 31-year-old woman, is the **Bijou Cafe**, 132 SW Third, Portland (223-3187). A 35-year-old woman enjoys going alone to small, intimate restaurants in northwest Portland for meals and company. "People talk to each other, as a rule" at the **Stepping Stone Cafe**, 2390 NW Quimby (222-1132), **Wheel of Fortune**, 1201 NW 21st (228-7528), and **Eat Your Heart Out**, 831 NW 23rd (222-6111) and in Portland neighborhood bars. **Coffee Ritz**, 921 SW Morrison (The Galleria), Portland (223-9649), for the same reasons, is a favorite of a 30-year-old woman.

Even shopping, people discover common interests. Specialty stores and specialty departments prompt strangers to talk, for example, about books or records they are considering. Small neighborhood businesses can be convivial meeting places, too—small stores or around the photoduplicating machines in print shops.

Grocery stores can be impulse meeting places. One woman finally got "positive results" from an attractive stranger (who had ignored her) after bumping him with her shopping cart. Cheese, wine, and spice selection may spark questions and prompt name and phone number exchanges.

Co-op groceries represent an earlier era of self-sufficiency and the small, gossipy neighborhood business. Shoppers often know one another; strangers readily talk among themselves. For those with a limited income and a taste for fresh, organic food, light labor in these stores translates into discount prices, too. Nonmembers, who pay full prices, are made to feel welcome at the following:

Food Front, 2675 NW Thurman, Portland (222-5658).

People's Food Store, 3029 SE 21st, Portland (232-9051).

Hope Co-op, 2017 21st, Forest Grove (357-5016).

Milk and Honey Non-Profit Food Store, 18930 SW Boones Ferry Rd., Tualatin (692-0925).

Good Neighbor Food Co-op, 175 SE Second, Hillsboro (640-1007).

Good things have been known to happen in laundromats. Yes, laundromats. Mutual boredom can lead to sharing refreshments nearby while the machines whir.

If these seem too mundane, try St. Patrick's Days. Bars have boisterous, sardine-like atmospheres, a 32-year-old woman recognizes. Celebrants go from bar to bar, turning up bubbly new acquaintances everywhere. That can take hours, if you're strong enough.

Public events connected to hobbies abound, and are often free. Certain hobbies attract more men than women, and vice versa; some attract specific age groups. A 49-year-old woman discovered the first principle by attending her first antique car show and tour: "tons of single men." She would also expect to find many men checking quotations in brokerage houses, and few seem in a hurry.

A mind-boggling number of benefits compete for your dollars. These dinners, dances, cocktail parties, auctions, rummage sales, performances, and sundry happenings cost from one to several hundred dollars. Cost and cause largely determine the crowds, and the atmospheres run from the warmly welcoming to the downright cliquish.

Businesses and public agencies also advertise free events, such as openings or anniversaries, where it's easy to end up talking with someone new. These events, with their free entertainment and refreshments, contests or giveaways, can become party-like in subdued ways. Choirs, strolling flute players, or comely models may confront you. Pick what appeals and drop in alone or with a friend for a bit of fun.

Bold? Try a slightly outrageous way of meeting people in a party mood. Check the Monday *Oregonian* or the magazine *Portland* for upcoming conventions. Drop in on their get-acquainted cocktail parties before main banquets. Pass quickly through them until finding a specially interesting person. Talk a bit, exchange names and leave.

ATHLETICS AND FITNESS

The YMCA, YWCA, and Mittleman Jewish Community Center have substantial offerings for single folk. Whatever their names, all are coeducational and open to everybody. (Also check the "classes" section for some of the many other services they offer.)

YMCA and YWCA units widely differ in the scope and size of their adult programs and facilities. Membership costs and fees vary from place to place. The YWCA does have an annual membership charge—halved if over 62—good at all YWCAs, but then may charge activities fees.

YMCA Metro Fitness Center, 2831 SW Barbur Blvd., Portland (223-9622) is primarily for adults, with family use mainly on weekends. According to a 38-year-old woman member, it "is a singles hangout as well as workout" place. Another woman who uses the jogging trail at adjacent Duniway Park describes frequently meeting attractive joggers entering from this Y. It has a lower membership rate for singles than couples.

YMCA Commonwealth Fitness Center, 421 SW Sixth, Portland (223-7643) has a fitness program and facilities designed for adults downtown. Anyone may belong—there's a lower rate for singles—or pay a daily use fee.

YMCA John R. Leach Center, 6036 SE Foster Rd., Portland (775-4396) has adult aquatic and exercise programs and facilities. Anyone may belong—with lower rates for singles—or pay for the activity.

YMCA Southwest Center, 398 N. State St., Lake Oswego (636-1212) similarly has a small adult program. Nonmembers pay for any activities.

YMCA Northeast Center, 1630 NE 38th, Portland (281-1169) has facilities and programs for adults in aquatics, fitness, sports, and dancing. There is only a membership fee.

Clark County YMCA, 1115 Esther, Vancouver (206-695-3414 or from Portland 289-3805; weekends 206-696-6181) has fitness programs and recreational sports and facilities and classes on a fee basis for members and nonmembers.

YWCA Downtown Center, 1111 SW Tenth, Portland (223-6281) offers numerous learning, personal development, health, and indoor and outdoor recreational facilities, classes, and opportunities, including tours. Most members are younger than 35. Its Women's Resource Center offers counseling, emergency aid, support groups, and career services. (See chapters 7 and 9.)

YWCA St. Johns Center, 8010 N. Charleston, Portland (286-5748) has a fitness center, classes, and support groups.

YWCA Northeast Center, 126 NE Alberta, Portland (288-5173) has personal development classes and support groups.

Vancouver-Clark County YWCA, 1115 Esther, Vancouver (1-206-696-0167) has personal development classes, counseling, and support groups for women. It also has classes, job assistance, and career counseling, some through its Women's Resource Center. (See chapters 7 and 9.)

Mittleman Jewish Community Center, 6651 SW Capitol Hwy., Portland (244-0111) has extensive facilities. It conducts an array of cultural, educational, recreational, and sports programs, activities, and classes. Singles get lower membership rates. Classes and many activities are open for the same or higher fees to nonmembers. MJCC has a singles group (see chapter 4) and a senior club.

Single people throng facilities and programs of park and recreation departments throughout the metropolitan area. In Vancouver, Hillsboro, Lake Oswego, and Portland, for instance, they run tennis and racquet centers which, like Portland's public golf courses, use mixers to match players unknown to one another. Portland's public racquet courts are **Portland Tennis Center**, 324 NE 12th, Portland (233-5959) and **St. Johns Racquet Center**, 7519 N. Burlington, Portland (248-5020). Also check the free seasonal guide of its **Outdoor Recreation Service**, 426 NE 12th, Portland (248-4018) for extensive offerings, some requiring preregistration.

Park and recreation departments in and out of Portland also operate swimming pools. Oregon City, for instance, has one, while Tualatin Hills Park and Recreation District has them in Aloha, Beaverton, and elsewhere. Seasonal park and recreation schedules are left in public places, mailed, or available from their public information offices.

Commercial physical fitness clubs advertise heavily for the singles trade. Young singles often picture them as providing recreation, fitness, and a place to meet other singles. Members play racquetball, swim, take saunas, use weight rooms, and otherwise exercise. Men and women congregate in exercise and relaxation areas.

Membership turnover, however, is high. The costs, the dashed social hopes, or both drive out many within a few months, a former spa official says. Some members remain steadfast, satisfied by the fitness possibilities alone. Before joining, make sure you feel at home in the club. Take advantage of any trial membership. Some racquet clubs offer certain privileges to nonmembers.

Portland State University, **Portland Community College**, and several hospitals also operate certain physical fitness programs open to the public. The hospitals are **St. Vincent Hospital and Medical Center**, 9205 SW Barnes Rd., Portland (Education Services, 297-4411), **Portland Adventist Medical Center**, 10123 SE Market, Portland (257-2500), **Providence Medical Center**, 4805 NE Glisan, Portland

(230-1111), and **Good Samaritan Hospital and Medical Center**, 1015 NW 22nd, Portland (Oregon Fitness and Health Center, 229-7006).

Private athletic clubs—all in the phone books—are costly; few have waiting lists. They typically have very good, often excellent facilities as well as classes and a variety of interest groups, especially for the recreation-minded.

If you like things athletic, says a 40-year-old woman who belongs to two private Portland clubs, they are worth joining; "you get an eclectic grouping" in them. "Try a cross-section of their activities. The more people you know, the more connections you will have with the opposite sex." Private clubs, she adds, have their own bar scenes, but the play seems mainly between married couples or people talking business.

CLASSES

Our region exemplifies what Ronald Gross in *The Lifelong Learner* calls "The Invisible University." It is chock-full of free and inexpensive learning options. Other parts of *Single in Portland* suggest how churches and synagogues, Y's, community centers, lectures, workshops, clubs and activities groups, parks, activist organizations, arts centers, and agency after agency enhance individual learning and personal development.

Consider other local segments of The Invisible University: growth centers (where you explore yourself, your emotions, and human relations); consciousness raising and support groups (see chapters 4, 6, and 7); correspondence study; tape cassettes on many subjects; learning groups and learning exchanges you may join or start; televised courses; simulation games; "open" college programs; and on and on.

All you need to get started is genuine curiosity or interest. Is there a subject that attracts you or a skill you have never pursued?

Classes and workshops may afford the quickest way to learn among other people. Ask a few questions beforehand: What is it you want to know or develop by enrolling? Will it create new experiences for you? Promote personal change or growth?

Stretch your imagination and knowledge? Add or deepen skills? Is it a place to meet someone sharing your interest? Will it be enjoyable? Is the teacher competent?

"Classes are excellent places for meeting people," a 36-year-old woman says. Thousands agree. Most feel that the experience will be most successful if you enroll in classes that genuinely interest you. It helps, too, to view classmates as people as interested as you are in enriching their lives, as creative folk, as doers. The assumption opens you to learning from them, not just the instructor. Seeing them as competitors usually does the opposite.

Expect some heavily male classes, including those concerned with computers and auto maintenance, and some heavily female, such as sewing classes. But surprises may be in store, as things are changing. Auto maintenance is attracting women. Cooking classes at **Portland Community College** are usually coed and attract a wide age range, says a 66-year-old man. "Cooking classes are good because you *do* things together." For him, that was more congenial than discussions, lectures, or classes, as in sculpturing, in which he had worked alone.

"PCC has a massage class that's great," reports a 33-year-old woman. Men pair off with men, women with women, to give one another massages—so everyone leaves feeling good—and everybody becomes well acquainted, she adds. "We went out for beers after classes."

Take your time and relax. Do not rush in and out of class. Arrive early or stay late to chat if you want to expand friendships. Going out afterward as a group for refreshment or entertainment can follow. Some instructors like joining out-of-class activities.

Classes are everywhere. Commercial enterprises teach a tremendous variety of skills: Community colleges are quick to introduce new courses as interests and tastes change. Also check with smaller colleges in the metropolitan region for their personal and professional development workshops, seminars, and programs. Meanwhile, here are two of the largest sources of non-credit classes:

Portland State University, 1633 SW Park, Portland (229-

4800 or Oregon toll-free 1-800-452-1368) is the biggest continuing education program in Oregon. Some 25,000 enroll annually. Its quarterly catalog is jam-packed with liberal arts, business, science, and all manner of professional development opportunities. Independent study is also available. Classes, workshops, and seminars also meet in Beaverton, Gresham, Lake Oswego, Milwaukie, Oregon City, Tigard, Vancouver, and West Linn.

Marylhurst College for Lifelong Learning, Marylhurst (636-8141 or 224-5828) has many enrolled "seeking to enhance their lives through non-degree programs." Many are women. Classes mainly are in the liberal arts, in its Prior Learning Experience program, and in a few professional development sectors. Much teaching happens nights and weekends, typical of classes in this book section. A handful of classes also meet in Beaverton, Wilsonville, and downtown Portland.

A mix of practical knowledge and appreciation of the arts, sciences, nature, or technology characterize the many non-degree classes and workshops at **Pacific Northwest College of Art**, 1219 SW Park, Portland (226-2811), across at **Northwest Film Study Center** (221-1156), at **Oregon School of Arts and Crafts**, 8245 SW Barnes Rd., Portland (297-5544), **Western Forestry Center**, 4033 SW Canyon Rd., Portland (228-1367), across at the **Oregon Museum of Science and Industry**, 4015 SW Canyon Rd., Portland (222-2828), and nearby at **Hoyt Arboretum**, 4000 SW Fairview, Portland (228-8732).

OMSI, Western Forestry Center and Hoyt Arboretum also lead outings and field trips. **Washington Park Zoo**, 4001 SW Canyon Rd., Portland (226-1561) offers classes, outings, and field trips related to wildlife. **Outward Bound School**, 0110 SW Bancroft, Portland (243-1993) offers classes, outings, and trips related to skiing, rafting, camping, and mountaineering.

Consider, too, smaller or less-well-known opportunities:

American Red Cross, PO Box 70, Portland 97207 (Eve, 243-7712) teaches kayaking and canoeing.

Center for Urban Education, 0245 SW Bancroft, Portland (221-0984) has classes, workshops, and conferences on topics related to social change, the church, and public communication for nonprofit organizations.

Pacific Northwest Labor College, 1529 SW 12th, Portland (226-3326) is open to all workers. It offers workshops and programs in occupational safety and health, and union topics.

Red Rose School, 5215 NE 30th, Portland (George or Cris, 282-7812) offers classes and study groups from a "politically left perspective" on history, political theory, arts and culture, current events, and practical skills which further social action.

৵

Community schools (see below), community centers, and parks and recreation programs present an amazing array of low-or no-cost "leisure education" opportunities. Their classes and workshops enhance cultural, recreational, and personal development interests. Their extensive schedules may change seasonally; card nights and dance exercise classes may be year-round, but rafting and skiing lessons are not.

A 27-year-old man reports that for singles the community centers "are great places to meet people and quite good for expanding your interests and finding new ones." Heavy single participation is common at many centers and in many park and recreation programs.

Portland operates the region's largest community school and park and recreation programs. You can learn various dances at several of the fifteen community schools, including the **Metropolitan Learning Center**, 2033 NW Glisan, Portland (241-0299). For the arts, try Park Bureau classes at the **Firehouse Theatre**, 1936 SE Montgomery, Portland (248-4737), **Theatre Workshop**, 511 SE 60th, Portland (235-4551), and **Community Music Center**, 3350 SE Francis (235-8222). Singles flock to its **Multnomah Art Center**, 7688 SW Capitol Hwy., Portland (248-3333). Its **Interstate Firehouse Cultural Center**, 5340 N. Interstate, Portland (243-7930) stresses ethnic performing, visual, and literary arts.

Smaller, but still diverse, Community School programs for adults are in the school districts of Battle Ground, Canby, Centennial, Corbett, David Douglas, Milwaukie, Gladstone, Oregon City, Molalla, Ridgefield, and West Linn. Heaviest users are Oregonians in the 35 to 45 year old range. Community centers, as in Vancouver, house comparable leisure education opportunities.

Anything popular is taught almost everywhere. Square dance clubs, recreation departments, community centers, and commercial studios all teach square dancing, for example.

For sailing lessons—some free—in the spring, choose from the sailing clubs, parks and recreation departments, Portland's **YWCA**, **Portland Community College**, **Portland State University**, **Reed College**, **Lewis and Clark College** (in Portland 636-8504), or **U.S. Coast Guard Auxiliary** (in Portland 644-6191). The last one also teaches power boating classes.

For some specialized classes, you just might have to do a little research. Only a tiny notice told me that the **Bicycle Repair Collective**, 1912 SE Ankeny, Portland (233-0564) teaches bike mechanics, including how to overhaul a bicycle.

It makes sense to follow through on a new or improved skill or interest by joining a club devoted to it. (See chapter 3 and, on how to find them, chapter 2.) Instructors often know about these clubs.

Some classes expressly are for singles. Typical titles are The Single Experiences, Relationships, Connecting, Rebuilding (after a divorce or separation), Understanding Men, Marriage Autopsy, How To Be Friends with the Opposite Sex, and Assertiveness Training (for which you don't need to be single). (For single parenting classes, see chapter 7.)

Classes for singles may show up almost anywhere. They are taught with some regularity at **Portland Community College**, **Clackamas Community College**, **SOLO Center** (see chapter 4), and **Open University**, 5289 Elam Young Parkway, Hillsboro (640-5678). Each has its classes in various locations.

Fresh information on classes, workshops, and seminars appear in catalogs, events calendars in print and broadcast media, ads, club and organizational newsletters, and published institutional schedules. Parks and recreation departments, community schools, and community centers issue seasonal schedules independently or together. *Willamette Week* prints twice-yearly educational sections. The annual *Portland Reflection*—and monthly *Transformation Times*—detail learning opportunities for those with new-age, personal growth, and holistic health concerns. Any of these sources can whet your appetite for new learning.

JUNE, 1983

LAST MONTH

May 1983
S	M	T	W	T	F	S
1	2	3	4	5	6	7
8	9	10	11	12	13	14
15	16	17	18	19	20	21
22	23	24	25	26	27	28
29	30	31				

S	M	T	W	T	F	S
			1	2	3	4
5	6	7	8	9	10	11
12	13	14	15	16	17	18
19	20	21	22	23	24	25
26	27	28	29	30		

NEXT MONTH

July 1983
S	M	T	W	T	F	S
					1	2
3	4	5	6	7	8	9
10	11	12	13	14	15	16
17	18	19	20	21	22	23
24	25	26	27	28	29	30
31						

SUNDAY
156/209
5

1 pm Take Betty's kids to zoo

MONDAY
157/208
6

Intro Session at SOLO Center   8 pm

TUESDAY
158/207
7

WEDNESDAY
159/206
8

Aunt Anne's birthday party — bring present   8 pm

THURSDAY
160/205
9

Begin exercise program at home   DO IT!

FRIDAY
161/204
10

Parents without Partners Dance   9 pm

SATURDAY
162/203
11
● NEW MOON

JUN. 5 TO 11, 1983

7
SINGLE PLUS

SINGLE PARENTS

Single parents experience all the pains and pleasures of single life—and then some. Children bring rewards and frustrations usually unknown to the childless. Single parenting presents unique social, emotional, and monetary complications.

As a group, single parents have far fewer *organized* resources available than their immense number require. Mutual support among single parents becomes particularly important, then. They must look to their own devices and to personal qualities to cope with and master changed, perhaps unexpected conditions.

"Boy, am I glad I was wrong about my chance of making it on my own," says a 39-year-old single parent. Hers is a common sentiment among single parents about new-built assertiveness and competency. "Having always been dependent and never having been encouraged or 'trained' in habits of independence," she says that she chose divorce only as a last alternative. "I like myself much better than I did, feel more confident about myself" as a single and single parent after "learning things that I had never had a chance to 'get out' when I was a 'daughter' or a 'wife.'" The main disadvantage of singlehood has been letting herself "ask for help when I need it without the great fear of losing this independence."

As a single person and single parent, she continues, "My strongest new friendships have grown with people of similar interests or similar lifestyles—other divorced women making it on their own." From such feelings of kinship, many single parents develop mutual support.

Single parents here involve themselves in the very same groups, events, and places described elsewhere in *Single in Portland*. They are noticeably in singles clubs, with or without their children. The SOLO Center (see chapter 4), in its special concern for those divorcing or separated, attracts many single parents. Churches and synagogues may have single parent support groups.

Organizations below also furnish opportunities for single parents to gather with others from one-parent households:

Parents Without Partners has five metropolitan chapters. (See chapter 4 for their locations.) PWP is a social and educational organization for single parents, custodial or not, of living children. There are groups for members' teenagers, too.

After using a free, time-limited Courtesy Card, single parents must join PWP to participate. Any single may attend its popular monthly dance. (See chapter 5.)

PWP balances adult, family, and educational activities. Members share experiences, make new friends, lend mutual aid—especially emotional support—and take part in various activities. One member writes that "the personal growth experienced by our active members is the best measurement" of PWP success.

The 278-member Portland chapter, largest of the five, has one or more events *daily*. "Adult" events include "happy hours," card parties, volleyball, house parties, restaurant visits, and dancing. "Amigo" potlucks and small group discussions are for new members and Courtesy Card holders. They feature "friendship, a listening ear, a lot of encouragement to feel at home and to get involved." Coffee-discussions and similar educational events are frequent. "Family" gatherings include volleyball, hot dog and movie nights, birthday parties, holiday celebrations, bowling, hikes, roller skating, pizza feeds, and boat trips. And there are orientation, membership, and other meetings, too.

Portland PWP members range from their mid-twenties to their fifties. Most are in their thirties and forties. The majority are women.

Children Deserve Support, c/o Women's Resource Center, 19241 S. Beavercreek Rd., Oregon City (656-2091) is a new mutual aid organization for custodial parents interested in changing laws involving child support. It educates members and others and lobbies public officials and agencies about child support.

Hinson Baptist Church, 1137 SE 20th, Portland (Rev. Lauterbach, 232-1156) has a Sunday School class, retreat, and other activities for single parents younger than 35 and a comparable group for single parents older than 35.

Non-Custodial Parents Association of Oregon, 13385 SW 115th, Tigard (639-7447) is a 200-member mutual aid, educational, legal, and lobbying group. It stresses equity and justice in domestic relations laws and works for children sharing the lives and love of both parents. Its special concerns are custody, child support, and visitation problems and issues. The association features rap sessions and other activities. Men and women alike belong.

Other groups with special concern for single parent members are **Association of Formerly Married Catholics** (see chapter 4), **New Life Soul Support**, and **Widowed and Young Support** (both in "widowed" section).

Several **YWCA** branches have women's centers (see chapter 6 and also "pregnant singles" section) which offer classes, groups, and other resources to single parents. (Also see "jobs" in chapter 9.)

Parenting classes, say single parents, can be quite useful as long as you do not turn them into occasions to wallow in self-pity or to seek a date or mate. These classes also develop into "tremendous support groups," according to one of their teachers.

School districts may offer parenting and single parenting classes at different locations during the school year. You can hear about these classes in the **Portland School District** by contacting Carolyn Sheldon at 249-2000, ext. 214. Community colleges, major hospitals, youth service centers, mental health and family service agencies, and the YWCA all teach parenting classes or workshops. **Clackamas Community College** has a credit course on part-time parenting. **YMCA**

East County Youth Service Center, 2057 SE 122nd, Portland (255-3338) and **Tigard Youth Services**, 11981 SW Pacific Hwy., Tigard (620-2621) offer single parenting classes. **Lutheran Family Service**, 605 SE 39th, Portland (231-7480) conducts a workshop on single parenthood open to all.

For further information, see "Parenting" and other monthly sections in *The Portland Family Calendar*. Also see the events calendars and announcements in the local press.

OLDER SINGLES

By choice or circumstances, many older people are single. If healthy, age doesn't keep you from joining in the same groups and events or going to the same places described elsewhere in this book. Still, many older people prefer to spend time among those near them in age. Among your opportunities are the following:

American Association of Retired Persons, 921 SW Morrison (Galleria), Rm. 417, Portland (227-5268) is the biggest of its many metropolitan Portland chapters. Ask them for other Oregon chapter contacts. For Vancouver, contact Hilda, 1008 U St., Vancouver (1-206-693-6247). AARP is for anyone over 55 years of age. Chapters sponsor a truly vast range of classes, community service projects, social gatherings, and entertainment, such as bowling and tours. Members have their own low-cost Portland pharmacy to use in person or by mail.

Elderhostel, Marylhurst College for Lifelong Learning, Marylhurst (Dr. M.A.F. Ritchie, 636-8141) is one of 500 American academic institutions providing short-term, low-cost academic programs for older adults. During spring and summer, participants live for five days on the Marylhurst campus, taking special non-credit courses. Changing weekly, these are in such areas as creativity, communication, art, music, medicine, mathematics, literature, drama, folkdancing, and personal development. No special background is needed, and there is neither grading nor homework. For programs outside Portland, write Elderhostel, 100 Boylston St., Suite 200, Boston, MA 02116.

Odyssey Club, 2101 NE Flanders, Portland (233-9961 or Oregon toll-free 1-800-452-4100) is a nonprofit membership club for anyone 50 years and older and for the disabled of any age. It conducts escorted recreational trips of local, regional, national, and international scope. These include matinee and evening performances, holiday lodge weekends, dinners at historical sites, and extensive tours. Pickup and return transportation is provided in Multnomah, Clackamas, and Washington counties.

æ

A number of local employers, including schools, government agencies, utilities, and some occupational groups, such as teachers, run retirement clubs. These usually combine social and entertainment functions with community projects and other activities.

Senior Centers throughout the metropolitan area welcome anyone 55 (sometimes, 50) and older. Their programs promote the physical, emotional, and financial well-being of participants. Meals, classes, dancing, singing, crafts, counseling, health checkups and maintenance, cards, games, conversations, musical groups, tours, holiday events, and the sharing of resources are typical activities. Groups spring from centers. For instance, **The Marshallaires**, 1514 B Date St., Vancouver (1-206-695-6047 or 1-206-693-8554) is a singing group which performs in the Vancouver area. Men and women, many single, use the senior centers daily.

Dancing to live music draws crowds to senior centers, and dancers find willing partners. Dances with Big Band live music are at **Friendly House Senior Service Center**, 1819 NW Everett, Portland (224-2640) on Wednesday afternoons. **Oregon City Senior Center**, 615 Fifth, Oregon City (655-8335) has its dances Tuesday evenings and Sunday afternoons. And **Eagles Lodge**, 4904 SE Hawthorne, Portland (232-7505) invites older persons to ballroom and pattern dancing on Saturday afternoons. (For other dancing, see chapter 5.)

Matt Dishman Center, 77 NE Knott, Portland (282-1460) has old-time dancing with live music Monday noons and Thursday noons. **Mount Scott Community Center**, 5530 SE

72nd, Portland (774-8156) has the same on Tuesdays. **Luepke Senior Center**, 1009 E McLoughlin Blvd., Vancouver (1-206-696-8202) has old-time dancing every first and third Sunday afternoon.

To locate the nearest senior center, call **Information and Referral Service** in Portland at 222-5555. *The Yellow Pages* and *The Portland Women's Yellow Pages* list some, but not all.

Senior clubs are even more plentiful. Public and private agencies, and many institutions, such as churches, run them throughout the metropolitan region. Ask at the nearest senior center for an appropriate senior club.

Senior centers and senior clubs often are good places to learn about the many special programs, events, and groups designed specially for older people. Local community centers, community school programs, park and recreation departments, and Y's all sponsor them.

Senior Job Center, Portland Community College, 12000 SW 49th, Portland (244-6111, ext. 582) helps those wanting full- or part-time temporary or permanent work. It matches jobs with applicants over age 50, including those who have never worked before, such as widowed housepersons. It also conducts occupational testing, job counseling, and career workshops or refers clients to appropriate ones. All services are free.

Older men and women may use the YWCA's **Flexible Ways to Work**, 1111 SW Tenth, Portland (241-0537). It promotes flexible work options, including job-sharing and part-time and flex-time work, and offers job bank listings and an information exchange.

For house and apartment sharing services, see the final chapter.

WIDOWED

Losing a spouse is a traumatic entry into singlehood. Most widowed persons are over 50 years old; the great majority are women. Some, however, are younger and have young children.

Several local groups help ease the first shock, then offer further free aid to the widowed. In most groups, members themselves counsel the newly widowed. These groups have low-key social events and usually sponsor informative speakers.

Association of Formerly Married Catholics, with several chapters, includes widowed persons. (See chapter 4.)

New Life-Soul Support, St. Henry Catholic Church, 346 NW First, Gresham (Sister Phyllis, 666-3791) is a Tuesday evening support group for Catholics and non-Catholics experiencing widowhood, divorce, or separation. It helps reintegrate them into parish life. The group has occasional social events. The seven to 15 belonging are mostly between 25 and 50 years old.

Parents Without Partners, with five chapters, has widowed members. (See "single parents.")

Sounding Board for Widows and Widowers, c/o Portland State University Adult Learning Center, PO Box 751, Portland 97207 (229-4739) gathers 50 to 60 widowed persons the second and fourth Mondays each month for speakers and for restaurant luncheons. It has a confidential counseling program.

Survivors Offering Solace (SOS), 5512 SE 73rd, Portland (771-1321 or 221-1054) is for anyone who has lost a loved one from sudden death. It holds monthly rap sessions or small group discussions. Specially trained volunteer-survivors help the newly bereaved by phone or in person.

U.S. with PEACE, East Hill Church of the Foursquare Gospel, Gresham. (See chapter 4.)

Washington County Widow-Widowers, c/o Donelson, Sewell and Mathews, 171 N. Third, Hillsboro (Connie, 648-3158), in which survivors counsel the newly bereaved, meets monthly in Hillsboro for speakers and a social hour. It sponsors summer picnics and tours.

Widow-Widower Program, PO Box 407, Gresham 97030 (Stan, 665-4811) attracts from 30 to 50 persons monthly to educational and social programs. Widowed participants range upward from 30 years old, with most between 50 and 70.

Widow-Widower Program, c/o Gable Funeral Home, 225 NE 80th, Portland (253-7569) gathers monthly for speakers and social hours and, every third month, a potluck. Counseling is available.

Widowed Persons Service, American Association of Retired Persons, 921 SW Morrison (Galleria), Rm. 417, Portland (229-4739 or 227-5268) puts widowed individuals in touch with others who have experienced similar situations. Their trained volunteers talk to or visit the newly bereaved and discuss adjustment issues. Group sessions and telephone referral information and assistance are available.

Widowed and Young Support (WAYS), PO Box 407, Gresham 97030 (665-4811) is for the under-50 widowed, their families, and those working with bereavement groups. It usually meets monthly for rap and support sessions, speakers, resource-sharing, and social affairs. Up to 15 belong, mostly between 25 and 45 years old.

Widowhood Group, Milwaukie Center, 5440 SE Kellogg Creek Dr., Milwaukie (653-8100) is a weekly support group, except during summer, with a mental health professional leading it. Six or more widowed individuals participate, most older than 55.

The annual "Clubs and Organizations" Sunday supplement in late October to *The Columbian* lists a number of widowhood groups in the Vancouver area. As none answered my inquiries, I cannot verify their existence or provide details.

Men and women members of the YWCA who lost a loved one may join a twice-monthly support group at the **St. Johns YWCA**, 8010 N. Charleston, Portland (286-5748).

Portland Community College, 12000 SW 49th, Portland (244-6111) and **SOLO Center**, 4225 NE Tillamook, Portland (287-0642) offer widowhood adjustment courses.

DISABLED SINGLES

Single people with physical or mental disabilities have the same wants as other singles, as well as special needs brought on by the disabilities. Numerous opportunities exist locally for meeting these wants and needs.

Many organizations, places, and activities described in other chapters will be right for disabled persons. Contact them beforehand about particular suitability to your needs. Some groups may need a little educating; their participants often need to learn about the disabled as *individuals*, not solely as people with disabilities.

The Portland region has a full share of disability-tailored groups and activities. Local chapters of national organizations for the disabled form one big category. Often led by the disabled, they try to represent their interests, keep members up-to-date on policies, groups, programs, and events of interest, and further connections with the able-bodied. Most chapters have parties, picnics, outings, and other social events. These chapters are listed in Robin Jacob's book, *The Portland Guide for the Handicapped*, especially pages 127-130 and in her sections on alcohol and on the deaf. They are not repeated here. **Information and Referral** in Portland at 222-5555 will also identify chapters in the four-county metropolis.

The Greater Portland Association of the Deaf, 8134 N. Denver, Portland (289-0124; to add information, 654-3074 TTY) operates a TTY-Deaf Hotline. It identifies classes, recreational events, and other weekly activities.

For Clark County, contact **Coalition of Handicapped Organizations** (COHO), PO Box 5187, Vancouver 98668 or 611 Grand Blvd., Vancouver (1-206-696-6068 TTY or Voice). It has classes, support groups, and various activities.

The following organizations furnish recreational, social, or cultural opportunities for disabled men and women. Few of them charge. Fun, personal accomplishment and growth, knowledge, better feelings of self-worth, broadened friendships—these are their goals.

Able-bodied friends, families, volunteers, and staff often are active in them. Families can learn in this manner that the disabled can and do take risks and accomplish more than families anticipated.

For physical disabilities:

Beaverton Athletic Association for the Deaf. Call in Beaverton 641-6863 TTY.

Easter Seal Society, 5757 SW Macadam, Portland (228-5108) has both swimming for the disabled and the 59er's Rollin' Squares, a wheelchair square dancing group.

Flying Outriggers Ski Club (Janet, 281-7459 in Portland) is a three-track skiing club for any amputees or persons recovered from polio.

Forest Grove Swimming Program for the Handicapped, 2300 Sunset Dr., Forest Grove (357-7766).

Handicapped Sportsmen's Club, c/o Bill, 1634 SW Hensley, Troutdale (665-0149) mainly is a fishing group for those in wheelchairs. Members also go camping and attend rodeos together.

Hearing Impaired Ski Program, Multorpor Ski Bowl, PO Box 87, Government Camp (272-3522 Voice).

Independent Living Program, 521 SW 11th, Suite 306, Portland (224-9605) has an extensive physical and social recreation program for physically disabled, mobility impaired adults.

Northwest Outward Bound School, 0110 SW Bancroft, Portland (243-1993) offers a ski-mountaineering course for the hearing impaired.

Odyssey Club, 2101 NE Flanders, Portland (223-9961 or Oregon toll-free 1-800-452-4100) is a nonprofit membership club for the disabled of any age and for others over 50 years old. It conducts escorted recreational trips. (See "older singles.")

Oregon Bass and Panfish Club, PO Box 1021, Portland 97207 (282-2852), described in chapter 3, includes individuals with physical disabilities. Call beforehand to arrange wheelchair access to its regular meeting place.

Parcourse Outdoor Fitness Center for Disabled Persons, Portland Adventist Medical Center, 10123 SE Market (251-6108) has four exercise stations for those in wheelchairs able to exercise with their upper torsos.

Portland Athletic Club for the Deaf. Call in Portland 225-1096 TTY.

Portland Parks and Recreation Bureau Services for Disabled Citizens, 426 NE 12th, Portland (248-4328) has a big schedule of events (e.g., bowling, dancing, fitness, trips, drop-ins) slated at different places and times.

Portland Wheelblazers Wheelchair Athletic Association, 2082 NW 15th Ct., Gresham (Kathie, 661-1987) is a basketball team for those in wheelchairs or permanently unable to stand up.

Rio Rockets, c/o Rehabilitation Institute of Oregon, 2010 NW Kearney, Portland (229-7151) is a wheelchair track and field team.

Rollin' Rebels Wheelchair Sports Association, c/o Scott, 9691 SE 82nd, Portland (774-8861, ext. 13) is a wheelchair basketball team.

SOAR (Shared Outdoor Adventure Recreation), PO Box 14583, Portland 97214 (238-1613) has skiing, hiking, camping, bicycling, horseback riding, rafting, and other outdoor activities for the disabled jointly with able-bodied volunteers. "They will help you adapt the sport to your particular handicap and make it possible for you to do it on your own," says a participant.

Therapy Program, Mittleman Jewish Community Center, 6651 SW Capitol Hwy., Portland (244-0111) has a therapy pool and registered therapist for the physically disabled.

Tualatin Hills Park and Recreation District, 15707 SW Walker Blvd., Beaverton (645-6433) has an aquatic program for physically disabled adults (call 645-7454) and a therapeutic pool with therapists (call 643-6681).

Western Amputee Golf Association. Call Hal, 665-4442 h or 256-5330 w in Portland. This local chapter is for amputees to golf individually or together, including in tournament play.

Wheelies Bowling League, c/o Martha, 7146 SW Oleson Rd., Apt. 51, Portland (246-1189) is open to the physically disabled and able-bodied. Ten teams bowl September to April on Saturday afternoons at Milwaukie Bowl, 3056 SE Harrison, Milwaukie (654-7719).

YWCA Program for Special People, 1111 SW Tenth, Portland (223-6281) runs a personalized swimming program for the disabled.

Physically disabled individuals interested in horseback riding or horsepacking may contact Carl Hay, 627 SE 53rd, Portland (238-0049).

For therapeutic riding lessons, contact **Handicapped Equestrian Learning Program**, PO Box 358, Ridgefield, WA 98642 (1-206-887-8509 or 1-206-892-3286). For flying lessons, call Ken Foote, c/o Portland State University Flying Club at 245-6550.

For information on sports and recreational opportunities for the disabled, check the annual Oregon Paralyzed Veterans *Sports Review*, available for a contribution plus $1.50 mailing cost from Oregon Paralyzed Veterans Association, 3623 SE Hawthorne, Portland 97214.

és

For mental disabilities:

Recovery, Inc., 6731 N. Tyler, Portland (231-1334) also has chapters in Beaverton, Canby, Gladstone, Lake Oswego, Oregon City, and Vancouver. It is a no-cost, adult self-help group for "nervous persons" and former mental patients. Led by trained individuals who overcame these problems, the weekly meetings and phone calls emphasize mental health through structured will training.

Clubs exist for former mental patients, too. These help further the adult's potential and participation in community life. Each club below combines recreational and social opportunities with training in life skills. Their programs include conversation, games, sports, speakers, parties, and outings. Members are usually single.

These clubs are **Club 53**, 2617 NW Savier, Portland (228-4391), **David's Harp**, 11261 NE Knott, Portland (253-8883), and **Try-Angle Club**, 5215 N. Lombard, Portland (283-6955 drop-in center or 285-9871). "Try it once," advises a staff member. "If you like it, go back. If you don't, wait a while and try it again."

PREGNANT SINGLES

A single woman actually or possibly pregnant often feels very much alone. She wants first to determine if she is pregnant. Deciding what to do next involves complex issues and intense emotions if she is involuntarily pregnant. She wants support in the decisions she makes.

Various organizations, sensitive to the difficult circumstances, are ready to help at every stage. They usually charge nothing or relate fees to ability to pay. Find out details beforehand on how effectively a group follows through on promises.

The following organizations include abortion counseling or referrals in their services. Some of them also suggest alternatives to abortion.

Planned Parenthood, 3231 SE 50th, Portland (234-5411 until July 1983) and 1923 Broadway, Vancouver (1-206-694-1188).

Downtown Women's Center, 511 SW Tenth, Portland (224-3435 or 228-0246).

Outside-In, 1236 SW Salmon, Portland (223-4121).

Portland Feminist Women's Health Clinic, 6510 SE Foster Rd., Portland (777-7044).

YWCA Women's Resource Center, 1111 SW Tenth, Portland (223-6281).

Organizations which help while actively discouraging abortion are:

Abortion/Pregnancy Hotline, 11531 SE 30th, Milwaukie (239-4833).

Birthright Pregnancy Counseling, 4023 NE Halsey, Portland (249-5801).

Boy's and Girl's Aid Society of Oregon, 2301 NW Glisan, Portland (222-9661).

Right to Life Oregon, 534 SW Third, Room 812, Portland (222-3186).

※

Pregnant singles may draw upon local family counseling agencies and on **Parents Without Partners**, which welcomes unmarried parents. (See chapter 4.)

YWCA Women's Resource Center, 1111 SW Tenth, Portland (223-6281) conducts "Single Mothers' Support" for those in their twenties and thirties. It meets weekly for exercise, relaxation, group discussions, and information and resource-sharing. Child care is provided.

YWCA Women's Resource Center (above) also has a support group for women who ever had an abortion.

For other pre-natal and birth information, see the monthly "Pre-Natal" calendar in *Portland Family Calendar* and "Childbirth" in *Portland Women's Yellow Pages*.

EMERGENCIES

Facing a possible serious emergency in health, finances, or emotions is "the most terrifying aspect of being single," says a 36-year-old woman. "The prospect of facing a real crisis as a single and alone person," speculates a 34-year-old woman, is one reason "that people get married—to provide a built-in base of support that makes the world seem less threatening by facing it with someone beside you."

Portland singles face their emergencies in different ways. A 66-year-old man with grown daughters is sure that he would turn first to them, then to former wives with whom he enjoys good relations. "In spite of my desire to remain independent," writes a 39-year-old woman, "I have received loans from my parents (like when the cesspool caved in . . .) and am repaying them."

A 30-year-old man says, "When I was sick last year, friends looked in on me. When I was short of cash at times, my friends and family have lent me money. When I was emotionally distressed, I've had friends and family to call and talk to."

Faced with a financial crisis, another 34-year-old woman thinks that she would sell belongings and "borrow from an anonymous source (bank) rather than friends or family." Why make distinctions in emergencies? asks a recently separated 43-year-old man. "Call for help. What difference is there if one is single or married, or single with no family?"

By contrast, a 29-year-old man does make distinctions:

>If it were a serious health emergency, I'd probably rely on my folks.

>Emotional stuff is different. They'd be unlikely to understand, and probably be part of the cause. I'd reach out to my friends first.

>For financial emergencies, I'd go to my folks. I'd avoid going to them if I could find another way, though.

Friends or family, or even banks, are not always ready or able to help you through a serious emergency. In any case, locating help is as near as the phone.

Seven days a week, 24 hours a day, a trained person will help anyone calling a crisis line. He or she will talk to you about your crisis and may refer you to public or private agencies. This service is free and confidential. A crisis line is not a rap line.

Depending on where you live, call:

Metro Crisis Intervention Service (for Multnomah County) at 248-5430.

Clackamas County Crisis Line at 655-8888.

Washington County Crisis Intervention at 648-8636 or in Tigard at 248-3252.

Clark County Crisis Hot Line at 1-206-696-9560. A mental health professional is available days at 1-206-695-3416 and nights at 1-206-696-0165.

Portland Women's Crisis Line at 235-5333 for rape, sexual abuse, and harassment problems.

APRIL, 1983

S	M	T	W	T	F	S
					1	2
3	4	5	6	7	8	9
10	11	12	13	14	15	16
17	18	19	20	21	22	23
24	25	26	27	28	29	30

LAST MONTH

March 1983
S	M	T	W	T	F	S
		1	2	3	4	5
6	7	8	9	10	11	12
13	14	15	16	17	18	19
20	21	22	23	24	25	26
27	28	29	30	31		

NEXT MONTH

May 1983
S	M	T	W	T	F	S
1	2	3	4	5	6	7
8	9	10	11	12	13	14
15	16	17	18	19	20	21
22	23	24	25	26	27	28
29	30	31				

SUNDAY
114/251
24
10am Church Social Hour

MONDAY
115/250
25
Ask neighbors in for dessert

TUESDAY
116/249
26
Jane will call about person she wants me to meet

WEDNESDAY
117/248
27
○ FULL MOON

THURSDAY
118/247
28
Write Nelly & Sam about Summer visit

FRIDAY
119/246
29

SATURDAY
120/245
30
9 pm Dancing

APR. 24 TO 30, 1983

8

CLOSE ENCOUNTERS

FRIENDSHIPS

"Where are all the people I can have as friends?" To Edwards and Hoover in *The Challenge of Being Single*, that is the *real* question, not where can a single meet the one and only "special person."

"Making friends is what life is all about and life's most interesting and difficult activity," a 66-year-old man tells me. "It always has *risk* in it. We are all shy—no?"

Friends are good medicine for the spirit. With them, we share intimacies. For people who live alone, they are much, much more. Friends often form a network of human relations which takes the place of, or at least supplements, families.

A 34-year-old woman, who knew nobody when she came to Portland, remembers redefining the meaning of "her family" to embrace older people, children, couples, and single men and women. More than a dozen became her good friends. Together, they share "orphan dinners at holiday times" when it is easy to feel depressed. They "create a family environment with each other on special occasions" and share important rituals. Their friendships helped create what resembles a close-knit, multi-generation family.

Another woman took advantage of mass communications for much the same end. "Are you a single person, parent, grandparent, without family for holidays?" she asked in an ad. She wanted "to liven Christmas day for 91 y/o grandmother and myself by having 10-12 others join us for Christmas dinner." They had a ball, she recounts; several arranged to see one another again.

There is no set formula for friends. They may be of the same or opposite sex. They may be platonic or romantic attachments. They may be the same age as you, or older or younger. They may share your basic interests or be quite different.

Several singles here refer warmly to their platonic friends. "I can talk to them about anything—feelings, events, theories, other relationships—and we are there for each other," a 30-year-old man says. A 34-year-old woman seeks "their company without burden of other expectations (sex, commitment, emotional pendulum swings)" and enjoys the "absence of tension" in such relations. A 43-year-old man understands "relationships with women, my role in them, their responses and needs far better" after acquiring platonic women friends.

These, like any friendships, may entail risks. Platonic friendships helped teach a 31-year-old woman "to realize what I do seek in a permanent relationship." They are "disadvantageous when I feel there may be a spark of permanency that is not reciprocated." A platonic friendship, says a 34-year-old woman, is "quite an ego boost because it is a response to you as a person, not as a sexual object." When they work, "they're great for companionship and communication, and a male viewpoint," says a 36-year-old woman. When they work.

Friendships don't just happen. "I personally find it hard to get to know someone in the midst of a social situation, so I try to set up a one-to-one situation that is not so distracting, and where I don't have to compete for their attention," says a 29-year-old man.

"Close your eyes and jump," advises the 34-year-old woman. "Get used to introducing yourself at parties, at bus stops, at concerts and museums. It's always much easier to make new friends than I expect it to be."

Psychologist Stephen M. Johnson in *First Person Singular* suggests three basic guidelines for finding new friends: "First, pursue your own interests; second, keep your eyes open for promising acquaintances; and third, be persistent in your efforts to establish relationships."

A 24-year-old woman says:

"I'm getting more aggressive in pursuing women

friends. With men it's still a bit confused. More often than not they pursue me, and then we decide whether to go for friendship or a love affair. More to the point, friendship, *real* friendships with men are enabling me to trust and understand men and my reactions to them. It's important for me to see that there are men who can be open, accept criticism, and give affection and support without 'payment due.'

Friendships may be strengthened—or they may deteriorate. Separated for six months, a 43-year-old man has "kept in touch with married friends. There is nice continuity there, and some support." The 29-year-old man is sensitive to how a busy personal life threatens his friendships. "Still, if I reach out, even if it's just a call to say, 'I was thinking about you and wanted to know how you were doing and what's up,' it keeps things going" or at least maintains a mutual awareness which might "result in our getting together."

A 30-year-old man says of friendship in general: "You've got to give to get. It's that simple."

Many customary social patterns foster acquiring and improving friendships. Potlucks are favored ways in this part of the world to socialize with minimum fuss. "We get together for a Sunday lunch potluck once a month," a 33-year-old woman says of a group of men and women. "I look forward to them. There are always new people there." Afterwards, they check the Sunday paper and may go on to concerts together. Similarly, local clubs and organizations frequently combine potlucks with business meetings or programs. People meet comfortably in this manner.

The 29-year-old man loves to dance, so he takes advantage of the many local places and opportunities to dance. (See chapter 5.) It was at these dances that he first met several people who became friends. Meet such "people through people, organizations, and one's own interests," he concludes. "Get out and be as socially active as possible meeting people who like to do the things you like to do."

COUPLES

We live in a couples society, it often appears. There are parties which seem right out of Noah's Ark: two by two. Some neighborhoods seem the same way.

Those who are paired and those who are single often have only bare contact with one another. "I find that married friends have less time than single people do," a 36-year-old woman remarks. "My best friend recently got married, and I see her less and less now, so I just think I can't expect to see my married friends much. This is a big loss for me."

But is the loss inevitable or, if it happens, can it be reversed? Near-isolation of singles from the paired may happen by choice. It may, however, exist because of unexamined habits. Judgmental stereotypes—couples as "stodgy," singles as "selfish" or "swingers," for example—can widen this separation. Unhappy age stereotypes may lengthen the gap further. A 66-year-old man reports older married friends have a "romanticized" view of him, exaggerating "the gadabouting that I do and the excitement which comes from moving around a lot in different social activities."

There are married women who view single women as potential threats to their husbands' affections. A divorced woman encounters "paired women afraid I am after their men." They view single women as being "on the make." So "I neutralize it by being very friendly toward the *women*."

Instances of friendships between singles and couples are endless. Similarities of values, lifestyles, interests, experiences, or something else help form and reform their bonds. A single person may be friends with either or both the husband and wife. No one—neither a spouse nor a date—need be in tow to enjoy time with a friend.

A 29-year-old never-married man finds that his expectation that couples *want* friendships with singles leads to mutual payoff.

> I think people who are coupled realize more these days how important it is to maintain their friendships with other people outside the family, for vari-

ety and a fresh perspective, and also a much needed outlet for some feeling which might be too explosive to discuss much with their partner. For me, it feels really safe to be with someone who is coupled, and it makes me feel special. Also, when I'm with both partners, I get to see what life is like on the other side for future reference.

The 66-year-old man refers to couples in their thirties as not especially casual friends, but, by his preference, not especially intimate ones, either. He joins them, with or without a date, for picnics and special anniversary events, "and we have quite an enjoyable time." Period.

There may be all sorts of consequences, expected or not, from friendly relations with one or both persons in a couple. Free of any need to impress other singles, you can relax from any dating game you play.

A 30-year-old man "discovered a lot about children in the last three years" from married friends, "and I know how much more I want children of my own" as a result. He and they together learned about both single and married states. And "we have learned how to be independent as well as interdependent as friends/partners."

"Seeing how families function, solid relationships are created and maintained or fail is most important" to a never-married 24-year-old woman. Seeing how "children grow and friends wrestle with parenting is very special to me."

So couples may afford singles stability and reliability or alternatives to their present ways. They have taken in sick people who live alone and brought groceries, meals, and t.l.c. to many of them. A family holiday table is something many single people love sharing.

And singles have a lot to give paired friends. Some singles enjoy being a surrogate parent to friends' children or having them act the same way to their own. "I subscribe to the 'rent-a-kid' program—volunteering to take a friend's kid for an hour or a day." It "gives them a break and keeps me 'connected' with the nurturing side of my being," says a 34-year-old woman.

Certainly some couples may need gentle educating about

getting along with singles, or you in particular. They may be ignorant of singlehood or scared of becoming single. They may be as hesitant to intrude into what they consider a single person's terribly exciting life as you are into their time together. They may try to be too helpful, as in relentless matchmaking or advice-giving. Mutual relaxation may be needed in such cases.

THE PICKUP

"The hardest way to meet other single people is in normal, everyday activities," says a 28-year-old man. A familiar complaint? There those nameless, attractive creatures are—walking, shopping, eating, doing laundry, driving, standing in lines, sitting across a bus aisle or waiting room, almost everywhere.

Whether it is an everyday or out-of-the-ordinary situation, you want to stop staring and start meeting. If somebody present knows you both and volunteers (or with prodding, makes) an introduction, great. But you might not be so lucky.

The era when custom dictated that singles met only by formal introductions is over. So how about trying for a pickup? You are your own resource in this casual, unintroduced acquaintanceship. The pickup may be made with one or several hopes in mind. Forget the pickup done for exploitive, selfish, or unhealthy reasons. *Your* pickup is an act of friendship. It conveys your strong, worthy self. It is carried out in a friendly and uncontrived manner (even if a little quick planning went into it). Fantasize no longer. Sit there no longer thinking about it. Don't wait until others approach you. Do you want to choose— or wait always to be chosen?

Any man or woman may attempt a pickup. What do you have in mind? A day or evening together? A conversation to help decide what to do next? A possible sexual partner? Something which could become long-lasting? A combination of these? Something else?

The pickup is a highly customary social form among adults, according to *Singles*, a recent national survey. Simenauer and Carroll questioned 3,000 white, mainly middle-class singles between 25 and 55 years old about their single status.

Two-thirds of the men in their survey reported having tried to meet women by means of the pickup. Of these, one-third said that the majority of women responded positively to their attempts. Almost three-quarters of the women surveyed said that they would let a man pick them up if the place, time, and person met their standards. Strangely, the authors asked no women about their initiating pickups. Men are usually responsive, some even flattered, when it happens.

Pickups can happen at or near where people work. A 30-year-old man begins by smiling, joking, and light talk with attractive women "in the elevator, coffee shop, and entering and leaving" his big downtown Portland building. Of course, he must be prepared with a way to extend the encounter when either gets off the elevator.

Pickups may begin innocently with saying hello, asking a question, commenting on the weather or a happening, perhaps issuing a mild compliment. Introducing yourself is a simple way to begin. Transparent come-ons are resented. A nervous smile and signs of shyness rarely are. The important thing is to say something, almost anything, rather than play out a vignette in your head and do nothing.

"In situations like a dance where you have to choose a partner, I'd rather that someone else would take the initiative," muses a 29-year-old man. "I usually adopt a 'here goes nothing' attitude and plunge into uncharted waters, especially where I figure I don't have much to lose and might be pleasantly surprised (i.e., by someone accepting me, liking me, being open to contact)."

Direct or indirect signaling is a big help: smiles; direct eye contact; certain body movements. "Smile at someone who looks nice," advises a 32-year-old woman. That stranger often smiles back. By all means, keep eye contact.

"Someone good at picking up others is simply good at initiating conversation, adept at continuing it, and capable of asking for or signaling a desire for further contact," writes psychologist Johnson in *First Person Singular*.

You will be paying attention, real attention, to them as individuals in order to go beyond quick, shallow encounters. What are the positive features in one another, the humor, intelligence, shared interests and experiences, the achievements?

Friendliness is not always reciprocated. You will not please everyone, nor everyone, you. Unresponsiveness does not mean personal rejection. It may reflect the other's shyness—and suggest another gentle gambit to you. Fear of unresponsiveness should not discourage you from initiating pickups in appropriate settings.

Pickups follow no set outlines, and—unless both parties have the same one in mind—they have no determined result. Focus on the process of meeting and not the outcome. You may decide to meet later, exchange names and phone numbers, go somewhere together immediately, or move politely on to another person.

AT WORK

Some advice books caution singles against "office romances." Emotional entanglements supposedly deflate employee effectiveness and advancement. Even casual daters must concentrate on their work regardless of what goes on between them elsewhere. If one partner is rebuffed or the relationship sours, workplace harmony may suffer. Women who date male bosses, the books warn, invite sexual exploitation. These are points worth pondering.

Workplaces definitely are rich soil from which dates—friendships, too—may spring. Ten percent of the American men and nine percent of the women surveyed by Simenauer and Carroll in *Singles* reported meeting most of the people they dated at work. If the authors had asked whether they had *ever* dated someone met at work—among the public, customers, fellow or nearby employees—the percentages likely would have been much higher.

Employers often frown on employees dating customers they encounter. That never stops it happening, especially if done discreetly. Actually, many employers encourage employee socializing. Company clubs and functions, employee lunchrooms, holiday parties, and other occasions sponsored by employers are worth looking into.

Singles seeing each other week after week at work get a good look at one another. Prolonged encounters furnish valuable insights into one another, and any masks you or they wear for casual encounters probably slip away. Like what you see? Start getting to know those individuals outside work.

MAY, 1983

S	M	T	W	T	F	S
1	2	3	4	5	6	7
8	9	10	11	12	13	14
15	16	17	18	19	20	21
22	23	24	25	26	27	28
29	30	31				

LAST MONTH

April 1983
S M T W T F S
1 2
3 4 5 6 7 8 9
10 11 12 13 14 15 16
17 18 19 20 21 22 23
24 25 26 27 28 29 30

NEXT MONTH

June 1983
S M T W T F S
1 2 3 4
5 6 7 8 9 10 11
12 13 14 15 16 17 18
19 20 21 22 23 24 25
26 27 28 29 30

SUNDAY
128/237
8

Mother's Day   Dinner with mom.
respond to personal ads.

MONDAY
129/236
9

Place personal ad
          DO IT!

TUESDAY
130/235
10

WEDNESDAY
131/234
11

THURSDAY
132/233
12
● NEW MOON

Organize party circle
for week from Sat

FRIDAY
133/232
13

Check home sharing
opportunities

SATURDAY
134/231
14

MAY 8 TO 14, 1983

9
MOVING AHEAD

"Try everything. Don't look down your nose at something just because you already have an image of it." So says a 34-year-old Portland woman.

PERSONAL ADS

"Who Knows What Will Happen?" a local personal ad teased. The ad sponsors hoped to share "fun, companionable evenings" by bringing men and women together for dinners.

And seven women invited men another time to help bake and share Christmas cookies and rum "and meet new friends." "Come have a good time and meet new friends," promised the advertisers of a Halloween Party.

The personal classified advertisement is an underused avenue to broadening single life. Many more individuals consider placing or answering them than actually do so. Fear, distaste, or distrust of the medium steer them away. But personal ads have earned legitimacy in recent years. Popular publications have opened columns to them, barring or rewriting offensive and purely sexual come-ons. People have developed low-risk and high-reward ways of using ads.

Locally, people use ads for different reasons. Most advertise for potential companions, dates, or mates. "Am I really running an ad?" asks a man wanting a woman "who somewhat shares my world view and value system." "Looking for Mr. Right," asserts one; "for a good time but no perm. relationship," warns another; "for company," says a third. One Portland woman's ad drew more than 100 answers. Six months later, she had changed in goals and said as much. Advertising again drew far fewer, but still appropriate responses.

Through the ads people have formed bridge, folksinging, and "Happy Hour" bar groups. Some have recruited hiking, tennis, sailing, exercise, and travel partners or pen pals; others, members of support groups. Parties and potlucks are advertised, with or without prior screening by phone or letter. (See "Giving a Party.")

Personal ads are brief self-recommendations, accenting the positive. "Good woman hard to find? Not at all. Here's one," wrote one woman, who then illustrated why. If you have never assessed your personal qualities, designing a personal ad offers a prime opportunity. Also, it prompts you to think through what sort of relationship or connection you want.

The wording in the ad demands real thought. Many ads are too vague or uninformative, or shorter than their low cost warrants. Or they do not give quite the right information. If you've composed a trial ad, read it critically and ask yourself several questions. If "code words" are used, will readers understand their meanings? Those suggesting a chance to meet new "friends" at a party likely mean just that, but could be interpreted as offering sexual partners.

Ask, too, if the advertising medium has the sort of or enough readers you wish to reach. Do these readers live near or at a distance? Does it matter?

Those responding to ads should ask some questions of their own. Do advertisers genuinely note anything about their personalities, interests, concerns, aspirations, or feelings? What personal characteristics, such as age, health, or children, are spelled out? And what specifically do they demand or prefer in a compatible person or gathering?

Respond to what is actually said in an ad. Send a personal reply, not an obvious copy of one sent an earlier advertiser. Be sure to give your name and address or at least your name and phone number. Whether or not you enclose a requested picture is up to you.

Then talk at some length by phone before deciding whether you should meet. That way, neither of you will be unduly influenced by physical appearances. (An advertiser might consider holding back some likely possibilities among the replies as a backlog to contact later.) Don't hesitate politely to bypass anyone who does not sound "right." A Portland psychologist believes that phone screening helps separate out the secretly married and those operating from unhealthy fantasies from the single men and women who seek honest relationships.

Individuals normally then meet in public places, perhaps with a previously announced time limit. They may mutually decide to expand that time. New interest groups tend to gather first in homes, restaurants, or bars.

The following local media print nonexploitative ads and either blind box numbers or post office box numbers to protect advertisers' names and addresses. *Willamette Week*'s "Fresh Weekly" section has extensive ads. *SOLO News*, from SOLO Center (see chapter 4), has a monthly short selection. *Single Scene* monthly from Salem has classifieds for all Oregon. *Intro*, a national monthly magazine published in Los Angeles, has Oregon and Washington personal classifieds.

GIVING A PARTY

Giving a party is fun and a good way to extend friendships and meet new people. One need not be extroverted; the shy can give or cosponsor a party.

Why invite only singles or only those you know? Tell those coming to pass the word about the party to interesting people. Ask them to bring friends or loved ones. Organize a party circle. Each of five women, for example, can invite three men who are unknown to the other party-givers. Do it a second and third time with different men. The same method works for potlucks, dinners, and Sunday brunches. Try it at holiday times.

Let people know if you want to hear of parties to attend. Where are those sponsored by appropriate businesses, trades, or professions? Or by companies wanting your good will or business? Look, too, at the many organizations and groups in this book which have parties.

Some young professionals ran ads publicizing the parties they held as "a genuine alternative to the bar hustle and dating services" for those feeling "somewhat socially isolated simply due to lack of exposure to people whom you would like to meet." They offered refreshments, dancing, entertainment, prizes . . . and themselves. One organizer says that everyone seemed to have a good time, but that he wished more men would respond to such opportunities; women certainly did.

Several groups of women have invited fellow singles to a party by advertising in a newspaper. One group hired a downtown Portland hall and band and charged admission. Party games helped break the ice. Those attending without particular expectations apparently had the most fun, according to a woman present at two of these parties.

What party organizers did was set the scene: furnishing comfortable atmospheres for easily making acquaintances while people enjoyed themselves.

DATING SERVICES

Dating, or "personal introduction," agencies present themselves as dignified, quick, and safe ways to introduce individuals of similar background, interests, desires, likes, and dislikes. Clients seek companions, dates, or mates. Numerous companies advertise in local mass media and phone books. Those with addresses or phone numbers outside the region probably have clients outside the Portland area. Those with "club" in their title should not be confused with singles clubs, discussed in chapter 4.

These services are not totally without risk. This industry has a checkered past of trading on fantasies, financial chicanery, and undelivered promises. Owners admit that they cannot guarantee turning up that "special person" for you. Anyone— no matter their skill or qualifications—may begin dating services as businesses needing little investment. The agencies also claim satisfied customers. Expect them to accent positive accomplishments, such as the number of marriages for which they claim credit.

If you use one, consider choosing the least expensive. It probably has the most clients. This improves your chances of a compatible match, unless you are ready to meet just anyone. Only a service with hundreds of names on file is likely to produce even a short list of appropriate prospects. Ask how many are in the total client pool; if you don't get a straight answer, think about alternatives.

These companies typically choose the people you are permitted to consider. (Some permit browsing through albums of flattering, unidentified photographs.) Agencies may act as go-betweens to make certain parties mutually agree to meet. Anonymity continues until then.

Learn beforehand about all the personal factors a dating service considers important—and actually uses—from the material you provide. Some agencies include too few factors for anything but a rudimentary matching. Some agency owners admit to consulting their personal "intuition" before recommending matches. Determine, too, whether a computer dating service (which is probably more expensive) actually uses a computer. If so, does it use so few factors that it would be cheaper to match clients by hand? For agencies (even nonprofit ones) specializing in clients of similar religious background, ask the same questions. And, always, if you are asked to sign anything, be very careful.

The newest competitors for the dating service dollar are those using videotape interviews to help clients prescreen choices. Costs are higher, and the pool of choices is probably smaller than for non-video services. Clients discuss themselves and their preferences during videotaped interviews. They can view others' videotapes and will meet only by mutual agreement. Anonymity continues until then.

JOBS

"It is important to me to get some satisfaction from my career," writes a 36-year-old Portland woman. "Especially with no primary relationship, work satisfaction is more important." Hers is an often-expressed sentiment among singles. "Work is a major source of self-esteem," a 34-year-old woman argues.

After separating, "I used to work long hours to keep myself occupied," remembers a 30-year-old man. Divorce became a new beginning: a move "from the ranks of the employed to the ranks of the self-employed, a move I may not have made if I was still married. It has been one of the most enjoyable and self-satisfying things I have ever done."

Work, of course, affects a single person's income, self-respect, social standing, and future. "It's *tough to be unemployed* when you're single—there's no 'cushion' of a second income," adds, from experience, a 34-year-old woman.

"As a woman and single person, my career is an essential part of my identity, different from women who were trained to see marriage as their primary goal just a generation ago," says a 24-year-old woman. She continues,

> It keeps me out of depression—having goals and commitments apart from my relationships. Recently, I've taken the risk of leaving my job to pursue work more along the lines of my changing interests and am applying to graduate school.

If you are interested in finding, advancing in, or changing jobs, you may proceed in several ways. Local colleges furnish often free or inexpensive help through their career or life planning programs. Services include resource centers which emphasize self-help as well as workshops and seminars in career development, career change, and job searching. And they do career testing and counseling and teach related classes.

Contact one of the following:

Careers Program, Portland Community College, 12000 SW 29th, Portland (244-6111, ext. 406).

Career Development and Placement Center, Clackamas Community College, 19600 S. Molalla, Oregon City (657-8400).

Career and Life Planning, Mount Hood Community College, 26000 SE Stark, Gresham (667-7315).

Life Planning Center, Marylhurst College for Lifelong Learning, Marylhurst (636-8141).

Clark College, 1800 E. McLoughlin Blvd., Vancouver (1-206-694-6521).

The YWCA offers low-cost job and career aid through either of the following:

Flexible Ways to Work, 1111 SW Tenth, Portland (241-0537) promotes flexible work options, including job sharing and part-time and flex-time for men and women. It has job bank listings and an information exchange.

YWCA Job Bank, 1115 Esther, Vancouver (1-206-697-0167) helps women plan work force re-entry and career change. It provides job listings and career information.

In Portland, such Community Schools as **Atkinson** and **Binnsmeade** have job interviewing and job finding workshops. Check the Community Schools quarterly catalog, which is also printed in Portland Parks and Recreation Bureau seasonal schedules.

SOLO Center (see chapter 4) and various business, professional, and civic organizations (see chapter 3) also enlarge career and job skills. *The Yellow Pages* also contain enterprises which do it for a profit.

A single "displaced homemaker" may turn in several directions for aid. Consult one of the above career or life planning programs, call **SOLO Center** (see chapter 4), or **Tri-County Community Council** (which includes Clark County) in Portland at 222-5555. It will put you in touch with social service agencies.

"Use your friends and family. Ask them for money or for help finding you a job," suggests a career development specialist. "Don't expect to find an answer simply or easily. The important thing is, be tenacious. Keep at it."

HOUSING

Adult-only, singles-type apartment complexes are sparse in this area. They usually come equipped with extensive recreation and sports facilities included in the rent. The setup encourages residents to meet quickly and often—around pools, in saunas and gyms, on courts and trails. "Especially in warm weather, parties spill out into common areas, drawing people in," says a former resident of one such Portland complex.

Among the big adult complexes attracting many recreationally and socially active singles are:

McCormick Pier Apartments, 600 NW Front, Portland (287-7437).

Rock Creek Apartments, 18700 NW Rock Creek Circle, Portland (645-4444).

Tanglewood One (all adult) and **Tanglewood Two** (about half single), 4 SW Touchstone, Lake Oswego (636-0935).

Woodcreek Apartments, 3280 SW 170th, Beaverton (642-4055). About half single.

Those wishing to share an apartment or house may use the tested, time-consuming avenues: ads, posted notices, and word-of-mouth—all followed by interviews and checking references.

Or there are agencies which will, for a fee, bring people together by interests, lifestyles, and other standards. For instance:

Christian Roommate Service, Alderbrook Bldg., Suite 211, 2001 Main, Vancouver (206-693-8480 or from Portland, 225-1158) is related to a Christian dating service.

House Sharing Service, 4225 NE Tillamook, Portland (287-0642) matches housemates. See chapter 4 for its SOLO Center sponsor.

Housemate Register, 2405 NW Irving, Portland (225-1077) is a commercial agency.

Shared Housing, 519 SW Third, Portland (222-5559) is a social agency which matches compatible low- and moderate-income residents, including many older ones, so they can share owned and rented homes in Multnomah, Clackamas, and Washington counties. Services may be exchanged for housing. The agency charges a fee only if a shared housing arrangement is completed.

FURTHER READING

The Metropolitan Area

Virginia Church, Cheryl Lowe and Ann Wiselogle, *Portland By Bicycle* (Portland: Bicycle Commuter Service, 1982). A guide to scenic recreational tours through the city.

Carolan Gladden, *The First Book of Oregon Jazz, Rock and All Sorts of Music* (Wilsonville, OR: Hillman Publishing Co., 1982). Gladden found 165 clubs with music. She documents three dozen purely jazz clubs in the Portland area but has little to say on rock.

Michael Haughen and Richard Busch, *Portland After Dark: Book II* (Portland: H. B. Thumbs, 1980). One hundred and fifty area bars and clubs are evaluated, with descriptions of the predominant crowd, dollar values, service and drink quality, and delivery on advertised services, in this entertaining work. "Body exchanges" are noted. The book is partly outdated.

Connie and Terry Hofferber, *Portland Super Shopper* (Seattle: The Writing Works, 1983). "More than 400 places to buy for less."

Nancy Hutchins and Alice Meyer, *Portland in Your Pocket* (Portland: Incunabula Press, 1979). A guide to Portland.

Robin Jacobs, *The Portland Guide for the Handicapped* (Portland: Author, 1982). A specialized guide to the Portland area, but not to Clark County, and to national services, plus a bibliography. You may order for $7.95 including postage from PO Box 19471, Portland 97219.

Steve Johnson, ed., *The Portland Book: A Guide to Community Resources* (Portland: Center for Urban Education, May

1979). An information source, partially outdated, for over 2,000 organizations and government agencies and over 1,000 publications, reports, and periodicals relevant to metropolitan Portland.

The Junior League of Portland, Oregon, *Circling the City: A Guide to the Accessibility of Public Places in and near Portland, Oregon* (Portland: Author, 1978). A somewhat outdated, but still useful guide.

William Lamb, *Portland Off Beat Eaters' and Drinkers' Guide* (Portland: Ewe Me and Co., 1982). A pamphlet which notes the average age and type of patron and sometimes tersely describes some not especially offbeat places in a variety of categories. You may order for $2.95 postpaid from 921 SW Morrison, Suite 425, Portland 97205.

Linda Lampman and Julie Sterling, *The Portland Guide Book* (Seattle: The Writing Works, 1981). The third edition of a local guide book.

Multnomah County Library (Group Services), *Educational and Leisure Time Opportunities in Portland for Senior Adults 1980-1981* (Portland: Author, 1980). Partly outdated, this free pamphlet mainly describes Portland groups, agencies, and events exclusively of interest to older people.

An Open Door to Clackamas County (Marylhurst, OR: Association for Retarded Citizens of Clackamas County, 1981). A guide to physical access, food availability, and other aspects of a cross-section of public and private facilities. It is useful to anyone with physical disabilities.

John Perry and Buzz Willits, *Running Around Portland* (Portland: RAP Press, 1979). A guide to running-jogging routes in the Portland Vancouver areas.

Portland Women's Yellow Pages (Milwaukie, OR: Author, 1981) A directory of metropolitan women's (and some coeducational) skills, services, businesses, groups, and resources.

Peggy Robinson, *The Portland Walkbook* (Portland: Author, 1978) A guide to 50 areas in and within 30 miles of Portland that offer wilderness walks.

Tri-County Community Council, *Where to Turn: A Directory of Health, Welfare and Recreation Agencies* (Portland: Author, March 1982). A pamphlet directory to these agencies in the four metropolitan counties; free by calling 222-5555 in Portland.

Singles

Steven L. Atlas, *Single Parenting: A Practical Resource Guide* (Englewood Cliffs, NJ: Prentice-Hall, 1981). The title says it.

George Bach and Ronald Deutsch, *Pairing* (New York: Peter J. Wyden, 1970). A book of advice on increasing intimacy and bettering relationships.

Richard N. Bolles, *The Three Books of Life and How to Get Out of Them: An Introduction to Life/Work Planning* (Berkeley, CA: Ten Speed Press, 1978).

Richard N. Bolles, *What Color is Your Parachute? A Practical Manual for Job-Hunters and Career-Changers* (Berkeley, CA: Ten Speed Press, 1978). Two widely used books on their topics. They are often updated.

Boston Women's Health Book Collective, *Our Bodies, Ourselves: A Book by and for Women* (New York: Simon and Schuster, 1979). In this feminist work, see especially the chapters on sexuality and sexual relationships but also glance through the other chapters.

Buff Bradley, *et. al.*, *Single: Living Your Own Way* (Reading, MA: Addison-Wesley Publishing Co., 1977). Personal stories and published sources on coping with and in celebration of being single.

Lilly Bruck, *Access: A Guide to a Better Life for Disabled Americans* (New York: Random House, 1978). A somewhat dated, but still useful book.

Leonard Cargan and Matthew Melko, *Singles: Myths and Realities* (Beverly Hills, CA: Sage Publications, 1982). Two sociologists compare and contrast singles to non-singles in Dayton, Ohio, as to their lifestyles and outlooks. Their brief history of singles in the twentieth century United States is less useful.

Emily Coleman and Betty Edwards, *Brief Encounters* (New York: Doubleday and Co., 1979). "How to make the most of relationships that may not last forever."

Marie Edwards and Eleanor Hoover, *The Challenge of Being Single* (Los Angeles: J. P. Tarcher, 1974). A book of advice.

Ida Fisher and Byron Lane, *The Widow's Guide to Life: How to Adjust/How to Grow* (Englewood Cliffs, NJ: Prentice-Hall, 1981). A book of advice for widows.

Sherri Foxman, *Classified Love: A Guide to the Personals* (New York: McGraw-Hill Book Co., 1982). A light look at personal classified ads.

Barry and Linda Gale, *Discover What You're Best At: The National Career Aptitude System and Career Directory* (New York: Simon and Schuster, 1982). One of several useful books on the topic.

Richard H. Gatley and David Koulack, *Single Father's Handbook: A Guide for Separated and Divorced Fathers* (New York: Anchor Books, 1979). A book of advice for single fathers.

Dian Hanson, *How to Pick Up a Man* (New York: G. P. Putnam's Sons, 1982). Breezy advice from a sophisticated big city woman about developing chance encounters with men into friendships and perhaps something more.

Stephen M. Johnson, *First Person Singular: Living the Good Life Alone* (New York: J. B. Lippincott, 1977). This psychologist's sections on developing friendships, building intimate relations, and meeting people are particularly valuable.

Bryan M. Knight, *Single Parenthood* (New York: Van Nostrand Reinhold, 1980). A book of advice and resources for single parents.

Adeline McConnell and Beverly Anderson, *Single After Fifty: How to Have the Time of Your Life* (New York: McGraw-Hill Book Co., 1978). A book of advice.

Kristelle L. Petersen, *The Single Person's Homebuying Handbook* (New York: Hawthorne/Dutton, 1980). Outdated on financing but otherwise a useful book.

Letty C. Pogrebin, *Getting Yours: How to Make the System Work for the Working Woman* (New York: David McKay Co., 1975). A book of advice.

Martin Poriss, *How to Live Cheap But Good* (New York: American Heritage Press, 1971). A somewhat outdated but still helpful book.

Reader's Digest Fix-It Yourself Manual (Pleasantville, NY: The Reader's Digest Association, 1977). The title says it. One of many useful books on the subject.

Lynn Shahan, *Living Alone and Liking It: A Complete Guide to Living on Your Own* (n.p.: Stratford Press, 1981). A book of advice mainly for those new to singlehood.

Jacqueline Simenauer and David Carroll, *Singles: The New Americans* (New York: Simon and Schuster, 1982). A national unscientific survey of white, mainly middle-class singles from 20 to 55 years old.

Peter J. Stein, *Single* (Englewood Cliffs, NJ: Prentice-Hall, 1976). A sociological work, one of the first scholarly books on American singles.

Peter J. Stein, ed., *Single Life: Unmarried Adults in Social Context* (New York: St. Martin's Press, 1981). A book of readings on single life.

Isabella Taves, *The Widow's Guide: Practical Advice on How to Deal with Grief, Stress, Health, Children and Family, Money, Work, and Finally, Getting Back into the World* (New York: Schocken Books, 1981). A book of advice mainly for middle-class widows.

Donald M. Vickery, M.D. and James F. Frieds, M.D., *Take Care of Yourself: A Consumer's Guide to Medical Care* (Reading, MA: Addison-Wesley Publishing Co., 1976). A book with self-diagnosis charts and home treatment information for 68 common medical problems.

Martha Yates, *Coping: A Survival Manual for Women Alone* (Englewood Cliffs, NJ: Prentice-Hall, 1976). The book offers thorough coverage, although parts are outdated.

Bernie Zilbergeld, *Male Sexuality: A Guide to Sexual Fulfillment* (Boston: Little Brown, 1978). A psychologist offers descriptions and advice.

Leonard Zunin, *Contact: The First Four Minutes* (Los Angeles: Nash, 1972). A book of advice on establishing and strengthening human relationships during the first few minutes of an encounter with strangers, friends, and loved ones.

INDEX